CROSSING THE THREE T'S OF COOKING

Tried, Tested, and True

By
Mary Alice Conlin

112/250

MARSHALL - MICHIGAN
800PUBLISHING.COM

Crossing the Three T's of Cooking

Copyright © 2012 by Mary Alice Conlin

Cover design by Abbie Smith

Layout by Kait Lamphere

Author photo courtesy of author

The opinions expressed in this manuscript are solely the opinions of the author and do not represent the opinions or thoughts of the publisher. The author represents and warrants that s/he either owns or has the legal right to publish all material in this book.

ISBN-13: 978-1-937580-99-5

First published in 2012

10 9 8 7 6 5 4 3 2 1

Published by   2 MOON PRESS
                 123 W. Michigan Ave, Marshall, Michigan 49068
                 www.800publishing.com

All Rights Reserved. This book may not be reproduced, transmitted, or stored in whole or in part by any means, including graphic, electronic, or mechanical without the express written consent of the publisher except in the case of brief quotations embodied in critical articles and reviews.

PRINTED IN THE UNITED STATES OF AMERICA

ACKNOWLEDGEMENTS

Growing up on a dairy farm the youngest of fourteen children, I watched how my mother thoughtfully and creatively came up with three meals a day. Her desire was to please her family and she lovingly devoted her life of service to them. While reading through her diary in her early years of marriage, I was impressed with the simplicity that she viewed her career as a mother. Her goal was to ensure that her children were well taken care of and played happily. During my years as a teen I became enthralled with her Rumford cookbook and her Family Circle magazines, cutting out the recipes that someday I would try. Some of my fondest memories were going to her old kitchen cupboard and opening the doors revealing the stack of cookbooks housed on one side that were handed down to her from her mother, and on the other side were the fragrant Watkins spice cans. I received such inspiration from her. She taught me how to improvise recipe ingredients and scale up or down the portions as needed. I learned how to stretch a meal to accommodate unexpected guests. As I married and began raising my family, the lessons that I learned either by watching her in the kitchen or being taught step by step instruction, helped me to develop my own style of cooking. I realized that the importance of cooking for my family and entertaining guests with a meal were an integral part of the home. So, it is with pleasure that I dedicate this cookbook to my mother, my sisters, my husband and children. As I have taught my granddaughter to bow after her "performance" on the piano (she's only three), I bow to you and say thank you for your support in making my cookbook a reality.

**We're learning how to take a bow
after a job well done.**

Table of Contents

Introduction	1
Appetizers & Snacks	3
Breads	15
Cakes	33
Cookies	53
Desserts	69
Eggs, Cheese, Legumes	83
Fish & Shellfish	87
Meat	93
Pasta, Rice & Grains	115
Pies	131
Poultry	143
Salads & Dressings	159
Soups & Stews	185
Vegetables	205
Index	229

Introduction

Two years ago I realized that while I loved to search for new recipes or put a twist on an old one, I was constantly referring to my beat up recipe cards of my frequently used favorite recipes. I found that I was regularly giving out one of our favorites and often spent time searching everywhere to find it…was it in the card box or was it being used for a bookmark in one of my many cookbooks. I decided it was time to get the recipes all collected in one spot for easy access. Additionally, I wanted to pass on these favorites to my children. So, I decided to use my computer skills and start getting them organized. The result is the cookbook you are holding in your hands.

It represents a treasury of recipes that have been tried, tested, and have proven true to our family for more than forty years. What that means to me is that each time the recipe has been prepared, most of the time it has lived up to it's expectation and turned out as it did time and time before. Hopefully, you will find success in using them also. I would encourage all of you to try new recipes and develop your tastes. I used to think everything from scratch tasted so much better than quick and easier methods; however, I encourage you to do what works for you and your family. If you can substitute, improvise or change a method and still gain successful results, then go for it.

Our family members have enjoyed many dinners with our friends and loved ones. Many times our children would remember the times of happy dinner conversation with new and old friends gathered around good food. There were times that we stayed at the dinner table just laughing and sharing ideas long after the food had been devoured. So, begin cooking and invite someone over to sample your good results. It will be worth the effort.

Appetizers & Snacks

A favorite way to get a party started is to reach for some not so typical appetizers. Look for recipes that are simple to prepare and light enough so that appetites for dinner won't be ruined. Presentation is the key to success and by adding a few extra touches such as deviled eggs nestled on a bed of lettuce, you can make everything look luscious and inviting. Try using red, yellow, and green peppers that have been hollowed out for a festive look for your favorite vegetable dip. You might try a footed pedestal bowl to showcase your traditional holiday cheese ball. Speaking of the holidays, check out the recipe for Caramel Corn. It is awesome! Recently, my favorite appetizer has been the Asparagus Pesto dip with crackers. Remember simple touches make appetizers and snacks appealing.

Making Caramel Corn for the Christmas party.

ASPARAGUS PESTO

1 pound fresh asparagus spears, cooked
1/2 cup freshly grated Parmesan cheese
1/2 cup pine nuts or walnuts
1/2 cups olive oil
1 garlic clove, chopped
1 tablespoon lemon juice
1/4 teaspoon salt

1. Snap off and discard tough ends of asparagus. Cook asparagus covered in boiling water 3 to 4 minutes. Drain.
2. Plunge asparagus into ice water to stop the cooking process; drain. Coarsely chop asparagus.
3. Process asparagus, cheese, and remaining ingredients in a food processor 30 to 60 seconds or until smooth, stopping to scrape down sides as needed.
4. Serve with crackers.

Servings: 15
Yield: 2 1/2 cups

Cooking Times
Preparation Time: 18 minutes

Black Bean Salsa

1 15-ounce black beans drained and rinsed
1 can white corn drained
2 large tomatoes diced
1 large green pepper, finely diced
1 bunch green onions diced
2 teaspoons cumin
1 1/2 teaspoons sugar
2 tablespoons apple cider vinegar
Salt and pepper to taste
1/3 cup cilantro chopped

1. Mix all ingredients together, cover, and refrigerate at least 2 hours.
2. Serve with chips, tacos, burritos or chicken.

Servings: 15

Cooking Times
Preparation Time: 15 minutes
Inactive Time: 2 hours
Total Time: 2 hours and 15 minutes

CARAMEL CRUNCH

9 cups popped corn
9 cups of crispy cereal squares
1 cup slivered almonds, peanuts, walnuts, or pecans
1 cup butter
2 cups packed brown sugar
1/4 cup light corn syrup
1/8 teaspoon baking soda

1. Place popped corn, cereal, and nuts in a large heat proof pan.
2. Melt butter in medium sized pot. Add brown sugar and corn syrup.
3. Bring to a boil, reduce heat. Boil for 5 minutes.
4. Remove from heat and add 1/8 teaspoon baking soda.
5. Stir well. This will cause the mixture to foam and lighten in color. Slowly pour the hot mixture over the popped corn.
6. Spread on large sheet pans to cool.
7. Break into smaller clumps while still lukewarm.
8. Store in covered container.

Servings: 10
Yield: 20 cups

Cooking Times
Preparation Time: 5 minutes
Cooking Time: 5 minutes
Inactive Time: 5 minutes
Total Time: 15 minutes

Tips:

Try to have a partner to help for the pouring/stirring operation to more evenly coat the mixture.

Mixture is very hot, be careful when pouring and mixing the popcorn.

CHEESE BALL

2 8-ounce jars of blue cheese
1 8-ounce package cream cheese, softened
1 8-ounce package cheddar cheese
1 tablespoon minced onion
1 teaspoon Worcestershire sauce
1/2 cup crushed nuts

1. Grate cheddar cheese.

2. Mix all cheeses, onion, and Worcestershire sauce.

3. Shape into ball and roll in crushed nuts.

Servings: 15
Yield: 32 ounces

Cooking Times
Preparation Time: 15 minutes
Total Time: 15 minutes

Tips:
Cheese works best at room temperature.

CRAB MEAT SPREAD

1 8-ounce package cream cheese, softened
1 cup catsup
2 tablespoons horseradish
1 6-ounce package crab meat, drained

1. Spread cream cheese on serving dish.
2. Mix catsup and horseradish and spread over cream cheese.
3. Crumble crab meat on top of catsup mixture.
4. Serve with crackers.

Servings: 15

Cooking Times
Preparation Time: 15 minutes
Total Time: 15 minutes

Fruit Dip

1 cup marshmallow crème
1 8-ounces cream cheese, softened
1 teaspoon orange extract
1/4 teaspoon nutmeg

1. Combine all ingredients in bowl; mix well. Chill in refrigerator.
2. Serve with bite-sized fresh fruit on skewers.

Servings: 10
Yield: 32 tablespoons

Cooking Times
Preparation Time: 10 minutes
Inactive Time: 2 hours
Total Time: 2 hours and 10 minutes

Fruity Horseradish Cream Cheese

    1 8-ounce package cream cheese
    1/3 cup apple jelly, warmed
    1 tablespoon prepared horseradish
    1-1/2 teaspoon ground mustard
    1/3 cup apricot spreadable fruit
    Assorted crackers

1. Place cream cheese on a serving plate. In a small microwave-safe bowl, heat jelly until warmed.
2. Stir in horseradish and mustard until blended. Stir in spreadable fruit; spoon over cream cheese.
3. Serve with crackers. Refrigerate leftovers.

Servings: 10
Yield: Yield: 1-1/3 cups.

Cooking Times
Preparation Time: 10 minutes
Total Time: 10 minutes

GREEN PARTY RYE BITES

3 green peppers chopped
1 onion chopped
2 cups cheddar cheese grated
8 slices bacon cooked and crumbled
1 teaspoon Worcestershire sauce
1 teaspoon hot sauce
2 tablespoons horseradish
5 tablespoons mayonnaise
Loaf of party rye slices

1. Mix in large bowl and spread on party ryes.
2. Bake at 400° for 15 minutes.

Oven Temperature: 400°F

Servings: 25
Yield: 50 slices

Cooking Times
Preparation Time: 20 minutes
Cooking Time: 15 minutes
Total Time: 35 minutes

Hot Artichoke Dip

2 jars artichoke hearts chopped
1 cup mayonnaise
1 cup parmesan cheese, grated
Worcestershire sauce, to taste

1. Drain artichokes, chop.
2. Combine artichokes, mayonnaise, cheese and Worcestershire sauce.
3. Turn into lightly greased 1 quart baking dish.
4. Bake at 350° for 15 minutes.
5. Serve warm with assorted crackers.

Oven Temperature: 350°F

Servings: 10

Cooking Times
Preparation Time: 10 minutes
Cooking Time: 15 minutes
Total Time: 25 minutes

SALSA

8 cups diced tomato
1 tablespoon coarse salt
1 tablespoon coarse pepper
1/2 cup white vinegar
1 head garlic, peeled and separated
2 large onions chopped
4 jalapeno chilies, stemmed, seeded and finely diced
1 15-ounce can tomato sauce
1 green bell pepper seeded and chopped
1 red bell pepper seeded and chopped
1 yellow bell pepper seeded and chopped

1. Chop all vegetables.
2. Mix and let set for 30 minutes.

Servings: 24
Yield: 10 cups

Cooking Times
Preparation Time: 15 minutes
Inactive Time: 30 minutes
Total Time: 45 minutes

SMOKY EGGPLANT DIP

1 medium eggplant sliced in half lengthwise
1 tablespoon sesame seeds
2 tablespoons chopped fresh parsley
2 tablespoons olive oil
4 teaspoons lemon juice
1 clove garlic clove, minced
1/4 teaspoon salt

1. Heat oven to 400°.
2. Cut eggplant in half lengthwise and place, cut side down, on lightly greased baking sheet.
3. Bake eggplant 45 to 50 minutes or until tender and skin is blackened.
4. Set aside until cool enough to handle.
5. Meanwhile in small skillet, toast sesame seeds over medium heat, about 3 minutes or until lightly browned.
6. Peel eggplant; discard skin.
7. In food processor, with chopping blade, or large bowl, using potato masher or food processor, mash eggplant, parsley, oil, lemon juice, garlic and salt until just combined.
8. Transfer to a serving bowl and sprinkle with sesame seeds. Serve immediately or cover and refrigerate to serve chilled.

Oven Temperature: 400°F

Servings: 8
Yield: 1 1/2 cups
Cooking Times
Preparation Time: 5 minutes
Cooking Time: 45 minutes
Total Time: 50 minutes

Tips:

Minced garlic from the jar works great.

Breads

Tasty Rolls for hamburgers

My fond memories of watching my mother knead bread and the aroma that filled the air when the loaves came out of the oven, were an inspiration for me to pass onto my family. My mother would slice off the ends of the bread, known as the heel, and slather it with butter with nary a thought about calories or cholesterol. I think as a kid the first thing I learned to prepare was bread, butter, and cinnamon sandwiches. Before I was married, I joined a book club to receive cookbooks and the first one I received was a bread baking cookbook. It wasn't long before the smell of freshly baked bread filled my own kitchen and I gladly sliced off the ends of the bread and passed it out to my family. Try the hamburger rolls for your next cookout to make it special or the cinnamon rolls for that Saturday morning coffee with your significant other or for your next holiday dinner, try Grandma's rolls. They are a favorite request.

Grandma's Rolls

BREAD STICKS

3/4 cup milk
1 tablespoon sugar
2 teaspoons salt
1 tablespoon soft shortening
1 package yeast
1/4 cup warm water about 115°F
3 to 3 1/4 cups sifted all purpose flour

Bread Stick Topping

1 egg white
1 tablespoon water
Coarse salt

1. Scald milk. Remove from heat and add sugar, salt and shortening. Blend and cool to lukewarm.
2. Sprinkle yeast over warm water; stir to dissolve.
3. Add the milk mixture and 1 1/2 cups flour to the yeast. Beat with electric mixer at medium speed until smooth, scraping the bowl occasionally.
4. Add more flour, a little at a time, first with spoon and then with hand, until dough leaves the sides of the bowl.
5. Turn dough onto lightly floured board. Knead until smooth and elastic, about 8 minutes. Place in lightly greased bowl; turn dough over to grease top. Cover and let rise in warm place until doubled, about 45 minutes.
6. Turn dough onto board and roll a 16 x 6 rectangle. From wide side, cut into 1/2 inch strips. Roll each strip under hand to make pencil shapes. Dough strips will be 8" long. Place a little apart on 2 greased baking sheets.
7. Let rise in warm place 15 minutes. Brush sticks with topping.
8. Bake in hot oven (400 °) 10 to 15 minutes, or until golden brown. Cool on wire racks.

Oven Temperature: 400°F

Servings: 10
Yield: 32 bread sticks

Cooking Times
Preparation Time: 15 minutes
Cooking Time: 10 minutes
Inactive Time: 1 hour
Total Time: 1 hour and 25 minutes

Cinnamon Rolls

2 cups whole milk
1/2 cup vegetable oil
1/2 cup sugar
1 tablespoon active dry yeast
4 cups flour

1/2 cup flour
1/2 teaspoon baking soda (scant)
1/2 tablespoon salt
1/2 teaspoon baking powder (heaping)

Note: Use less butter as butter runs off the dough and use less cinnamon if preferred.

Filling
1 cup melted butter
3/4 cup sugar
1/2 cup cinnamon

1. Mix whole milk, vegetable oil and sugar in a pan. Scald to 150 degrees. Let cool until lukewarm. Sprinkle in yeast and let sit.
2. Then add 4 cups flour, stir mixture together. Cover and let sit for one hour.
3. Add 1/2 cup flour, baking powder, baking soda, and salt. Stir mixture together.
4. Sprinkle surface generously with flour and form a rectangle. Roll the dough thin maintaining a rectangular shape.
5. Drizzle melted butter over dough. Sprinkle with sugar and cinnamon. Roll the dough toward you.
6. Pinch the seam to seal it.
7. Grease foil cake or pie pans. Cut rolls 3/4 to 1 inch thick and lay in greased pans.
8. Cover the rolls and let sit for 30 minutes.
9. Bake at 400° for 15 to 18 minutes.
10. Drizzle the frosting over warm rolls after they come out of the oven.

Oven Temperature: 400°F

Servings: 30

Cooking Times
Preparation Time: 15 minutes
Cooking Time: 15 minutes
Inactive Time: 1 hour
Total Time: 1 hour and 30 minutes

Tips:
Try the maple frosting or any glaze recipe.

Cool Rise Honey Lemon Whole Wheat Bread

3 1/4 to 4 1/4 cups all purpose flour
2 packages yeast
1 tablespoon salt
1/4 cups honey
3 tablespoons softened margarine or shortening
1 tablespoon grated lemon peel
2 1/4 cups hot tap water
2 cups whole wheat flour
Salad oil

1. Combine 2 cups all purpose flour, undissolved yeast and salt in a large bowl. Stir well to blend.
2. Add honey, margarine and lemon peel.
3. Add hot tap water all at once.
4. Beat with electric mixer at medium speed 2 minutes. Scrape bowl occasionally.
5. Add 1 cup whole wheat flour. Beat with electric mixer at high speed for 1 minute, or until thick and elastic. Scrape bowl occasionally.
6. Stir in remaining 1 cup of whole wheat flour with wooden spoon. Then gradually stir in just enough remaining all purpose flour to make a soft dough that leaves the sides of the bowl. Turn onto floured board; round into ball.
7. Knead 5 to 10 minutes or until dough is smooth and elastic. Cover with plastic wrap and then a towel. Let rest 20 minutes. Punch down.
8. Divide dough into 2 equal portions.
9. Roll each portion into an 8 x 12 rectangle. Roll up tightly into loaves beginning at the 8 inch side. Seal lengthwise edge and ends. Tuck ends under.
10. Place in greased 8 1/2 x 4 1/2 x 2 1/2 loaf pans.
11. Brush surface of dough with oil. Cover pans loosely with waxed paper, and then plastic wrap.
12. Refrigerate 2 to 24 hours at moderately cold setting. When ready to bake, remove from refrigerator. Uncover.
13. Let stand 10 minutes while preheating oven.
14. Bake at 400° for 30 to 40 minutes.

Oven Temperature: 400°F

Yield: 2 loaves

Tips:
Brush baked loaves with melted butter.

Dill Parmesan Popovers

3 eggs at room temperature
1 1/4 cups milk room temperature
1 1/4 cups flour
2 tablespoons parmesan cheese
1 teaspoon dill weed
1/4 teaspoon salt

1. Mix ingredients until frothy. Pour batter into muffin tins.
2. Bake at 450° for 20 minutes.
3. Reduce oven to 350° and bake for 15 minutes longer.
4. Remove from oven and split with sharp knife to allow steam to escape.

Servings: 8

Cooking Times
Preparation Time: 10 minutes
Cooking Time: 35 minutes

EASY OVERNIGHT CINNAMON ROLLS

18 frozen dough dinner rolls
1/4 cup instant vanilla pudding mix
1 cup brown sugar
2 tablespoons cinnamon
3/4 cup raisins
1/4 cup melted butter, more if needed

1. Grease a bundt pan.

2. Place frozen rolls in the bottom of the pan. Sprinkle evenly with vanilla pudding mix, brown sugar, cinnamon and raisins. Evenly pour melted butter on top. Let pan sit in the oven (cold) overnight to rise.

3. In the morning, bake at 350F for 25 minutes.

4. Let rolls sit for a few minutes then turn out onto a serving plate.

Oven Temperature: 350°F

Servings: 18

Cooking Times
Total Time: 2 minutes

GRANDMA'S ROLLS

1 3/4 cups lukewarm water
2 packages yeast
1/2 cup sugar
1/3 cup melted shortening
1 egg

1/2 cup dry milk
1 teaspoon salt
1 teaspoon baking powder
4 cups flour

1. Dissolve yeast in lukewarm water and add sugar.
2. Mix in shortening.
3. Add beaten egg.
4. Combine dry milk, salt, baking powder and flour and add to yeast mixture.
5. Mix well and knead the dough until smooth and elastic. Form into rolls and place in greased pans just touching each other.
6. Let rise until doubled and bake at 350° for about 20 minutes.
7. After the rolls come out of the oven, brush them with a mixture of sugar and milk. (About 1/8 cup of milk with 4 tablespoons of sugar).

Oven Temperature: 350°F

Servings: 12
Yield: 2 dozen

Cooking Times
Preparation Time: 20 minutes
Cooking Time: 25 minutes
Inactive Time: 2 hours
Total Time: 2 hours and 45 minutes

OLD FASHIONED EGG BREAD

1 1/2 cups milk scalded
1/2 cup butter
2 teaspoons salt
1/2 cup sugar
2 packages yeast
1/2 cup water, lukewarm
2 eggs, beaten
9 cups flour

1. Pour the scalded milk over the butter, salt, and sugar. Cool. Dissolve yeast in the lukewarm water and let it stand until it bubbles, about 5 minutes.
2. Add the yeast and the beaten eggs to the cooled milk. Gradually add the flour, beating it in thoroughly. Do not add any more flour than is necessary to make an easily handled dough, as the bread should be light and tender.
3. Turn out onto floured board and knead until smooth and elastic.
4. Place in greased bowl, cover, and let rise until doubled in size, about 1 1/2 hours.
5. Punch down and turn onto a lightly floured board. Shape into 3 loaves and place in greased 8-inch loaf pans. Cover and let rise until dough is just to the top of the pans.
6. Bake in 425° oven for 10 minutes, then lower heat to 350° and bake 40 minutes longer, or until bread is done.

Yield: 3 loaves

Cooking Times
Preparation Time: 15 minutes
Cooking Time: 50 minutes
Inactive Time: 3 hours

Overnight French Toast

1/2 cup butter (1 stick)
1/2 cup brown sugar
1/4 cup honey
1 teaspoon cinnamon
1/2 cup chopped pecans, walnuts or raisins
1 1/2 loaves French bread or baguettes
3 cups milk
12 large eggs
1/2 cup sugar
2 teaspoons cinnamon
1 teaspoon nutmeg
1/4 cup butter (1/2 stick), melted
2 tablespoons sugar
2 tablespoons brown sugar
1 teaspoon cinnamon

Oven Temperature: 350°F

Servings: 12
Yield: 12 x 9 pan

Cooking Times
Preparation Time: 15 minutes
Cooking Time: 45 minutes
Total Time: 1 hour

Continued on next page

Overnight French Toast

1. Spray a 9 X 13-inch baking dish with vegetable spray and set aside.

2. In a small saucepan under low-medium heat, melt 1 stick butter, 1/2 cup brown sugar, honey and 1 teaspoon cinnamon together and stir until blended and sugar is dissolved. Stir in nuts or raisins. Remove from heat, and spread in bottom of the baking dish.

3. Slice bread into 1-inch thick slices, take the sliced loaf in your hands, keeping it whole, and place it in the pan on top of the butter mixture.

4. In a large bowl with an electric mixer, or a hand whisk, whip the milk, eggs, 1/2 cup sugar, 2 teaspoons cinnamon, nutmeg and butter until mixed well and frothy.

5. Pour the milk and egg mixture slowly over the bread, opening up the slices to allow the liquid to get in between the bread. Press down to make sure all the bread is wet. Cover with plastic wrap, and press down once more to assure all the bread is soaked. Refrigerate overnight.

6. Next morning, preheat the oven to 350 degrees F. In a small bowl, mix 2 Tablespoons sugar, 2 Tablespoons brown sugar and 1 teaspoon cinnamon. Remove the plastic wrap and sprinkle the Overnight French Toast with the cinnamon sugar.

7. Bake for 45 - 60 minutes or until bubbly and the middle of the French toast is done. Do not over bake. Remove from oven and let cool 15 minutes before serving.

Tips:

Overnight French Toast stays hot for quite a while! Cut and serve with pure maple syrup and whipped cream if desired.

This recipe can be divided in half and baked in an 8 x 8-inch pan.

Pizza Night Pizza Dough

1 package active dry yeast
1 1/4 cups warm water about 115°F
3 1/2 to 4 cups flour
1/2 teaspoon salt

1. Sprinkle yeast on warm water; stir to dissolve. Add 2 cup flour and salt. Beat thoroughly. Stir in remaining flour. Turn onto lightly floured board and knead until smooth and elastic, about 10 minutes.

2. Place in lightly greased bowl; turn dough over to grease top. Cover and let rise in warm place until doubled, about 30 minutes.

3. Turn onto board and knead just long enough to force out large bubbles. Divide in half. Roll each half to make an 11" circle. Stretch each circle to fit an oiled 12" pizza pan. Add filling.

4. Bake in hot oven (450°) 20 to 25 minutes. Exchange position of pans on oven racks once during baking to brown pizzas the same.

Oven Temperature: 450°F

Servings: 8
Yield: Makes 2 pizzas

Cooking Times
Preparation Time: 15 minutes
Cooking Time: 20 minutes
Inactive Time: 30 minutes
Total Time: 1 hour and 5 minutes

Puffed Oven Pancake with Apple Raisin Sauce

Puffed Pancake

2 tablespoons butter
3 eggs
1/2 cup flour
1/2 cup milk
1/4 teaspoon salt

1. Place butter in a 10-inch ovenproof skillet (cast iron works great).
2. Place in a 400° oven for 3 to 5 minutes or till butter melts.
3. In a bowl beat eggs with a rotary beater until combined.
4. Add flour, milk, and salt. Beat until smooth.
5. Immediately pour into the hot skillet. Bake about 25 minutes or till puffed and well browned.
6. Cut into wedges and serve with sauce.

Apple Raisin Sauce

2 large apples, peeled, cored and diced
3/4 cup apple juice, water or cider
1/3 cup raisins
2 tablespoons sugar
1/4 teaspoon ground cinnamon
Ground nutmeg
2 tablespoons cornstarch
2 tablespoons cold water
1 teaspoon butter

1. In a skillet combine 2 large cooking apples, peeled, cored and thinly sliced; 3/4 cup apple juice or water; 1/3 cup raisins, 2 tablespoons sugar, and 1/4 cup teaspoon cinnamon. Add freshly ground nutmeg.
2. Simmer covered till apples are just tender.
3. Stir together 2 tablespoons cornstarch and 2 tablespoons water. Add to apple mixture.
4. Cook and stir till thickened and bubbly.
5. Cook and stir 2 minutes more. Stir in 1 teaspoon butter. Keep warm.

Oven Temperature: 400°F

Servings: 4

Cooking Times
Preparation Time: 10 minutes
Cooking Time: 25 minutes

Sweet Dough for German Applesauce Cake

      2 cups warm milk
      1 package yeast
      1 tablespoon sugar
      1 teaspoon salt
      1/2 cup margarine
      4 cups flour
      1/2 cup brown sugar
      1/2 cup butter
      1 1/2 cups applesauce

1. Scald milk and cool.
2. Mix with yeast, sugar, salt.
3. Mix in 1 cup of flour, add margarine.
4. Add remaining flour and let rise in a greased bowl to double in size.
5. Punch down and let rise again.
6. Divide in half and roll into 2 rectangles.
7. Place one rectangle in greased rectangle pan.
8. Place brown sugar and a little flour on the bottom rectangle.
9. Spread applesauce across and place 2nd rectangle on top.
10. Bake at 375° for 35 minutes or until golden brown.

Servings: 10

Cooking Times
Preparation Time: 20 minutes
Cooking Time: 35 minutes
Inactive Time: 2 hours
Total Time: 2 hours and 55 minutes

TERRIFIC HAMBURGER BUNS

5 cups all-purpose flour
2 packages dry yeast
1 cup milk
3/4 cup water
1/2 cup vegetable oil
1/4 cup white sugar
1 teaspoon salt

1. Stir together 2 cups flour and the yeast. In a separate bowl, heat milk, water, oil, sugar and salt to lukewarm in microwave. Add all at once to the flour mixture, and beat until smooth, about 3 minutes.

2. Mix in enough flour to make a soft dough, 2 to 3 cups. Mix well. Dust a flat surface with flour, turn dough out onto floured surface, and let rest under bowl for about 10 minutes.

3. Shape dough into 12 slightly flat balls, and place on greased baking sheet to rise until doubled in size.

4. Bake in a preheated 400 degrees F oven for 12 to 15 minutes.

Oven Temperature: 400°F

Servings: 12

Cooking Times
Preparation Time: 20 minutes
Cooking Time: 15 minutes
Inactive Time: 45 minutes
Total Time: 1 hour and 20 minutes

VALENTINE CHERRY SCONES

4 cups flour
1/4 cup sugar
1 tablespoon baking powder
1/2 teaspoon salt
1/2 teaspoon baking soda
2/3 cup butter
1 1/2 cups buttermilk
6 tablespoons cherry jam
Red sugar crystals

1. Heat oven to 425°. Grease large baking sheet.
2. In a large bowl, combine flour, 3 tablespoons granulated sugar, the baking powder, salt, and baking soda.
3. With pastry blender or 2 knives, cut in butter until mixture resembles coarse crumbs.
4. Add buttermilk to dry ingredients and mix lightly with fork until mixture clings together and forms a soft dough.
5. Turn dough out onto lightly floured surface and knead gently 5 or 6 times.
6. With floured rolling pin, roll out to 1/2 inch thickness and cut with 4-inch heart shaped cookie cutter.
7. Lightly press trimmings together and re-roll to cut more scones.
8. You should have 12. Place 6 dough hearts on greased baking sheet.
9. Top each with 1 tablespoon cherry jam. Moisten edge of dough with water and place a second heart on top. Press along edges to seal. Sprinkle tops with reserved granulated sugar and if desired red sugar crystals.
10. Bake scones 15 to 18 minutes or until golden brown. Serve warm.

Oven Temperature: 425°F

Servings: 6

Cooking Times

Preparation Time: 20 minutes
Cooking Time: 15 minutes
Total Time: 35 minutes

Whole Wheat Heartiness Bread

1 cup whole wheat flour
1 cup all purpose flour
1 1/2 teaspoons baking powder
3/4 teaspoon salt
1/2 teaspoon baking soda
1 beaten egg
1 cup buttermilk
3 tablespoons honey
1 cup raisins
1 beaten egg white

1. In a large bowl, combine flours, baking powder, salt and baking soda.
2. Combine the beaten egg, buttermilk, and honey. Add egg mixture to flour mixture; stir just till moistened. Stir in raisins.
3. Turn dough out onto a greased baking sheet; pat with wet fingers to an 8-inch round (dough will be wet). Brush with egg white.
4. Bake in a 350° oven about 25 minutes or till golden brown and toothpick comes out clean. If necessary, cover with foil the last 5 minutes to prevent over browning. Serve warm.

Oven Temperature: 350°F

Servings: 16
Yield: 1 loaf
Cooking Times
Preparation Time: 10 minutes
Cooking Time: 25 minutes
Total Time: 35 minutes

Wondrous Waffles

2 1/2 cups all purpose flour
1 tablespoon plus 1 teaspoon baking powder
3/4 teaspoon salt
1 1/2 tablespoons sugar
2 large eggs
2 1/2 cups milk
3/4 cup vegetable oil
1 teaspoon grated nutmeg

1. Combine first 4 ingredients in a large bowl.

2. Combine eggs, milk, oil and nutmeg; add to flour mixture stirring with a wire whisk just until dry ingredients are moistened.

3. Cook in a preheated, oiled waffle iron until golden.

Servings: 5
Yield: Approximately 5 8-inch waffles

Cooking Times
Preparation Time: 7 minutes
Cooking Time: 8 minutes

ZUCCHINI BREAD

3 eggs
2 cups sugar
2 cups grated zucchini
1 cup salad oil
3 cups flour
1 teaspoon baking powder
1 teaspoon baking soda
1/2 teaspoon salt
2 teaspoon vanilla
1/2 cup chopped nuts

1. Beat eggs, sugar, grated zucchini, and salad oil until foamy.
2. Add the rest of the ingredients. Pour into loaf pan.
3. Bake in 350° oven for 1 hour and 10 minutes.

Oven Temperature: 350°F

Servings: 12
Yield: 2 loaves
Cooking Times
Preparation Time: 10 minutes
Cooking Time: 1 hour and 10 minutes
Total Time: 1 hour and 20 minutes

Cakes

Despite what my guests might think, I am no expert when it comes to troubleshooting what might go wrong with baking cakes, but there is one procedure that I picked up along the way that works for me. After I bake a layer cake, I immediately wrap each layer in waxed paper and then freeze each one in its own freezer bag. When I am ready to assemble the layer cake, I simply unwrap each one and begin frosting the frozen layers. I let the cake thaw after it is decorated. This method has seemed to result in great tasting moist cakes. I once held a tea party where I served five different kinds of layer cakes using this method and each one was a hit.

This is Cherry cake for my niece's wedding shower. The cake stand was a gift for her.

APPLE HARVEST CAKE

1 1/4 cups white flour
1 cup whole wheat flour
1 cup sugar
3/4 cup brown sugar
1 tablespoon cinnamon
2 teaspoons baking powder
1 teaspoon salt
1/2 teaspoon baking soda
3/4 cup cooking oil
1 teaspoon vanilla
3 eggs
2 cups chopped apples
3/4 cup nuts if desired

1. Preheat oven to 325°.
2. Generously grease and flour 12 cup fluted pan.
3. Lightly spoon flour into measuring cup, level off.
4. In large bowl, blend all ingredients. Beat 3 minutes at medium speed.
5. By hand, stir in apples and nuts.
6. Pour into prepared pan.
7. Bake for 50 to 60 minutes.

Oven Temperature: 325°F

Servings: 12
Yield: 1 bundt pan

Cooking Times
Preparation Time: 10 minutes
Cooking Time: 50 minutes
Total Time: 1 hour

Awesome Cheesecake

Crumb Topping

1 1/2 cups crushed graham cracker crumbs
2 tablespoons sugar
2 tablespoons melted margarine

1. Mix together crumb topping ingredients and pat lightly into bottom of pan.
2. Save some for the top of the cheesecake.

Cheesecake

4 8-ounce packages of cream cheese
2 pints sour cream
2 cups sugar
2 teaspoons vanilla
6 eggs

1. Mix cheese until smooth, add sugar and blend well.
2. Add eggs, one at a time.
3. Add sour cream and vanilla. Mix well. Pour over bottom crumb crust.
4. Sprinkle top with reserved topping crumbs. Bake at 375° for 45 minutes (place in center of oven).
5. Keep oven door closed and turn off oven and keep cake in oven for 1 hour.
6. Remove from oven and cool and refrigerate overnight in pan.

Oven Temperature: 375°F

> **Servings:** 12
> **Yield:** 1 cheesecake
>
> ***Cooking Times***
> Preparation Time: 15 minutes
> Cooking Time: 45 minutes
> Inactive Time: 1 hour
> Total Time: 2 hours

Tips:

You may use canned pie filling for the top of the cheesecake.

CARAMEL GLAZE FOR STICKY BUNS

1/2 cup sugar
1/2 cup firmly packed brown sugar
1/2 teaspoon salt
1/2 pound unsalted butter
1/2 cup corn syrup
1 teaspoon lemon extract

1. In bowl of electric mixer, combine sugars, salt and room temperature butter.
2. Cream together for 2 minutes on high speed with the paddle attachment. Add corn syrup and lemon extract. Continue to cream for about 5 minutes, or until light and fluffy.
3. Use as much as you want to cover the pan of sticky buns with a 1/4 inch layer.

Servings: 16
Yield: 2 cups

Tips:
You may use this glaze if you do not have powdered sugar.

CARROT CAKE DRIED FRUIT RING

1 cup vegetable oil
1 cup white sugar
1 cup packed brown sugar
4 eggs
3 cups finely grated carrots
2 1/2 cups all-purpose flour
2 teaspoons baking powder
1 teaspoon baking soda

2 teaspoons ground cinnamon
1 teaspoon salt
1 cup raisins
1 cup candied cherries, halved
1 cup candied mixed fruit
1 cup dates, pitted and chopped
1 cup chopped walnuts
1/2 cup all-purpose flour

1. Preheat oven to 325 degrees F.
2. Grease and flour one 10-inch tube pan.
3. Beat the vegetable oil with the white and brown sugars.
4. Beat in the eggs one at a time. Stir in the grated carrots. Add the 2/12 cups flour, baking soda, baking powder, ground cinnamon, and salt. Stir until just moistened.
5. Toss the raisins, candied cherries, candied mixed fruit, chopped dates, and the chopped walnuts with the remaining 1/2 cup flour.
6. Stir to coat.
7. Add fruit and nut mixture to the batter and stir until combined.
8. Pour batter into the prepared pan.
9. Bake at 325 degrees F for 90 minutes.

Oven Temperature: 325°F

Servings: 14

Cooking Times

Preparation Time: 10 minutes
Cooking Time: 1 hour and 30 minutes
Total Time: 1 hour and 40 minutes

CUP CAKES

1 1/4 cups plus 2 tablespoons flour 1/3 cup shortening
1 cup sugar   2/3 cup milk
2 teaspoons baking powder   1 teaspoon vanilla
1/2 teaspoon salt   1 large egg

1. Heat oven to 400°.
2. Line 18 muffin cups with papers.
3. Sift dry ingredients into bowl. Add shortening, milk, vanilla.
4. Beat 2 minutes medium speed on mixer.
5. Add egg. Beat 2 minutes more.
6. Pour into baking cups filling 1/2 full.
7. Bake 15 to 18 minutes.

Creamy Frosting

3/4 cup milk   3/4 cup margarine (a little under)
Pinch salt   3/4 cup sugar (a little over)
4 tablespoons flour   1 teaspoon vanilla

1. For frosting, combine milk, salt, and flour over medium heat until it thickens.
2. Beat sugar, shortening and vanilla (5 minutes).
3. Add cooled mixture and beat 2 minutes more.
4. Frost cupcakes.

Oven Temperature: 400°F

Servings: 15
Yield: 18 cupcakes

Cooking Times
Preparation Time: 15 minutes
Cooking Time: 15 minutes
Total Time: 30 minutes

German Chocolate Cake with Coconut-Pecan Frosting

Cake

1 4-ounce bar sweet baking chocolate
1/3 cup water
1/2 cup butter (no substitutes), softened
1 cup sugar
1 teaspoon vanilla
3 egg yolks
1 2/3 cups all purpose white flour
1 teaspoon baking soda
1/2 teaspoon salt
2/3 cup buttermilk
3 egg whites stiffly beaten

Oven Temperature: 350°F

Servings: 12

Cooking Times

Preparation Time: 15 minutes
Cooking Time: 30 minutes
Inactive Time: 10 minutes

Continued on next page

German Chocolate Cake with Coconut-Pecan Frosting

1. Break chocolate bar into small pieces; add to water in a small saucepan. Stir over low heat until chocolate is melted. Remove from heat; cool to room temperature.
2. Cream butter, sugar, and vanilla in large bowl. Add egg yolks, one at a time, beating well after each addition. Blend in chocolate. In a separate bowl combine flour, baking soda, and salt; add alternatively with buttermilk to creamed mixture, beating after each addition until smooth.
3. Fold in beaten egg whites. Pour into two greased and floured 9-inch round cake pans.
4. Bake at 350° for 30 to 35 minutes or until cake tester inserted comes out clean.
5. Cool 10 minutes; remove from pans. Cool completely on wire racks; fill and frost with Coconut-Pecan Frosting.

Coconut-Pecan Frosting

2/3 cup evaporated milk
2/3 cup sugar
1/4 cup butter
1 egg, lightly beaten
1 cup coconut
1/2 cup chopped pecans
1/2 teaspoon vanilla

1. Combine evaporated milk, sugar, butter, and egg in a saucepan. Cook and stir over medium heat until thickened and bubbly, about 12 minutes. Add coconut, pecans, and vanilla.
2. Cool until thick enough to spread, beating occasionally.

Tips:

You may substitute sour milk for buttermilk by using 2 teaspoons vinegar plus milk to equal 2/3 cup.

Luscious Four-Layer Pumpkin Cake

1 package yellow cake mix (2 layer size)
1 15-ounce can pumpkin, divided
1/2 cup milk
1/3 cup vegetable oil
4 large eggs
1 1/2 teaspoon pumpkin spice divided

1 8-ounce package cream cheese, softened
1 cup powdered sugar
1 8-ounce frozen whipped topping
1/4 cup caramel topping
1/2 cup pecans, chopped

1. Preheat oven to 350°.
2. Grease and flour 2 (9-inch) round cake pans.
3. Beat cake mix, 1 cup of the pumpkin, milk, oil, eggs and 1 teaspoon of the pumpkin pie spice in a large bowl with electric mixer on medium speed until well blended.
4. Pour evenly into prepared pans.
5. Bake 20 to 22 minutes or until toothpick inserted in centers comes out clean.
6. Cool completely on wire racks.
7. Meanwhile, beat cream cheese in small bowl with electric mixer on medium speed until creamy.
8. Add powdered sugar, remaining pumpkin and remaining 1/2 teaspoon pumpkin pie spice; mix well.
9. Stir in whipped topping.
10. Remove cake layers from pans; cut each layer horizontally in half with a serrated knife.
11. Stack the layers on a serving plate spreading the cream cheese mixture between layers.
12. Do not frost the top layer.
13. Drizzle with caramel topping and pecans. Store in refrigerator.

Servings: 16

Cooking Times

Preparation Time: 15 minutes
Cooking Time: 22 minutes
Total Time: 37 minutes
Oven Temperature: 350°F

MAPLE FROSTING

1 bag powdered sugar
2 teaspoon maple flavoring
1/2 cup milk
1/4 cup melted butter
1/4 cup brewed coffee
Pinch of salt

1. Mix all ingredients.
2. Mixture should be thick but still able to pour.

Servings: 30
Yield: 2 cups

Cooking Times
Preparation Time: 5 minutes
Total Time: 5 minutes

Mini Black Forest Cakes

1 recipe for chocolate cupcakes
1 16-ounce cherry pie filling
1 container frozen whipped topping
1 jar maraschino cherries, for garnish
Chocolate shavings

1. Make cupcakes using a homemade recipe or box mix.
2. Bake in ramekins or cupcake tins.
3. Freeze cakes for individual preparation of Mini Black Forest Cakes

To assemble cakes:

1. Slice cakes in half and cut off a sliver from the bottom so that the cakes sit flat.
2. Put one half of the cake on a plate; scoop 2 tablespoons of cherry pie filling on top.
3. Place second half on top and add a dollop of cool whip and maraschino cherry. Garnish with some chocolate shavings.
4. Continue to assemble for the number of servings needed.

Servings: 12

Cooking Times
Preparation Time: 10 minutes
Cooking Time: 20 minutes
Inactive Time: 2 hours
Total Time: 2 hours and 30 minutes

Oatmeal Cake

Cake

1 1/2 cups boiling water
1 cup oats
1/2 cup butter
1 cup brown sugar
1 cup white sugar

2 eggs
1 1/3 cups flour
1 teaspoon soda
3/4 teaspoon cinnamon
1/2 teaspoon salt

1. Pour water over oats and let stand 20 minutes.
2. Cream butter, brown sugar, white sugar, and eggs and add to oatmeal.
3. Add flour, soda, cinnamon, and salt.
4. Mix and pour in 13 x 9 inch pan and bake for 30 minutes at 350°.

Broiled Topping

4 tablespoons butter
1/2 cup brown sugar
2 tablespoons milk
1 cup coconut
1 cup chopped nuts

1. Mix butter, brown sugar and milk. Bring to a boil and add 1 cup coconut and nuts.
2. Pour over warm cake and broil slowly until golden brown.

Oven Temperature: 350°F

Servings: 15
Yield: 13 x 9 inch pan

Cooking Times
Preparation Time: 15 minutes
Cooking Time: 30 minutes
Inactive Time: 20 minutes
Total Time: 1 hour and 5 minutes

Pistachio Cake

1 yellow cake mix (2 layer size)
1 small package instant pistachio pudding
4 eggs
1/2 cup oil
1 cup sour cream
1/4 cup water
1/4 cup sugar
2 tablespoons brown sugar
2 teaspoons cinnamon
1 cup walnut pieces

1. Mix all ingredients and pour half of the batter in a greased bundt pan.

2. Mix brown sugar, cinnamon, and walnuts on top of batter.

3. Pour the other half of batter on top of sugar walnut mixture.

4. Bake 45 minutes at 350°.

Oven Temperature: 350°F

Servings: 8

Cooking Times
Preparation Time: 10 minutes
Cooking Time: 45 minutes
Total Time: 55 minutes

PUMPKIN ROLL

3 eggs
1 cup sugar
2/3 cup pumpkin
3/4 cup flour
1 teaspoon soda
1/2 teaspoon cinnamon

1. Beat eggs, sugar, flour mixed with soda, pumpkin and cinnamon.
2. Line oblong cake pan with parchment or waxed paper. Pour cake batter on top of paper.
3. Bake at 350°.
4. Turn onto dish towel, roll up; refrigerate.
5. Unroll and top with filling.

Pumpkin Spice Cream Cheese Filling

1 6-ounce package cream cheese
1/2 cup butter
2 teaspoons vanilla
4 cups sifted powdered sugar (may need to add a little more for spreading consistency)
1/4 teaspoon Pumpkin Pie Spice

1. Mix all ingredients in a mixer.
2. Spread mixture on cooled pumpkin roll.
3. Re-roll filled cake and wrap in plastic wrap. Refrigerate.

Oven Temperature: 350°F

Servings: 10
Yield: 1 roll

Cooking Times
Preparation Time: 15 minutes
Cooking Time: 15 minutes
Inactive Time: 30 minutes
Total Time: 1 hour

STRAWBERRY RHUBARB COFFEE CAKE

Filling

3 cups sliced rhubarb, (1 inch pieces) fresh or frozen
2 quarts fresh strawberries, mashed
2 tablespoons lemon juice
1 cup sugar
1/3 cup cornstarch

1. In a large saucepan combine rhubarb, strawberries and lemon juice. Cover and cook over medium heat for about 5 minutes.

2. Combine sugar and cornstarch; stir into strawberry rhubarb mixture. Bring to a boil over medium heat, stirring constantly until thickened; remove from heat.

Oven Temperature: 350°F

Servings: 24

Cooking Times
Preparation Time: 15 minutes
Cooking Time: 45 minutes
Total Time: 1 hour

Continued on next page

Strawberry Rhubarb Coffee Cake

Cake

    3 cups all-purpose flour
    1 cup sugar
    1 teaspoon baking powder
    1 teaspoon baking soda
    1/2 teaspoon salt
    1 cup butter or margarine cut in small pieces
    1 1/2 cups buttermilk
    2 eggs
    1 teaspoon vanilla extract

1. In a large bowl, combine flour, sugar, baking powder, baking soda and salt. Cut in butter with a pastry blender until mixture resembles coarse crumbs.

2. In a separate bowl, beat together buttermilk, eggs and vanilla; stir into crumb mixture. Spread half of the batter evenly into a greased 9x13x2-inch baking dish. Carefully spread filling over the batter. Drop remaining batter evenly over filling with a tablespoon.

Topping

    1/4 cup butter or margarine
    3/4 cup all-purpose flour
    3/4 cup sugar

1. In a small saucepan over low heat, melt butter. Remove saucepan from heat; stir in flour and sugar until mixture is crumbly then sprinkle over batter. Lay foil on lower rack to catch any juicy fruit spillovers. Bake at 350° for about 45 minutes or until cake is done.

2. Cool cake in pan on rack. Cut rhubarb coffee cake into squares to serve.

Texas Sheet Cake with Fudge Frosting

Cake

2 cups flour
2 cups sugar
1/2 teaspoon salt
1 teaspoon baking soda
2 eggs

1/2 cup sour cream
2 sticks butter
4 tablespoons cocoa
1 cup water

1. Combine flour, sugar, salt, baking soda, eggs and sour cream.
2. Bring butter, cocoa and water to a boil. Add the boiling mixture to the flour mixture.
3. Cream well and pour into a greased 11 x 17 inch baking sheet.
4. Bake at 350° for 20 minutes.

Fudge Frosting

1 stick butter
6 tablespoons milk
4 tablespoons cocoa

1 box powdered sugar
1 cup walnuts

1. For the frosting, combine butter, milk and cocoa and boil for one minute.
2. Add 1 box powdered sugar blending with electric mixer.
3. Add walnuts. Spread on cooled cake.

Oven Temperature: 350°F

Servings: 24
Yield: 11 x 17

Cooking Times
Preparation Time: 15 minutes
Cooking Time: 20 minutes
Total Time: 35 minutes

WAKKY-KAKE

1 1/2 cups flour
1 cup sugar
3 tablespoons cocoa
1 teaspoon salt
1 teaspoon soda

1 teaspoon baking powder
1 teaspoon vinegar
1 teaspoon vanilla
5 tablespoons melted shortening
1 cup cold water

1. Mix flour, sugar, cocoa, salt, soda, baking powder all together. Make 3 holes.

2. In 1st hole put 1 teaspoon vinegar.

3. In 2nd hole put 1 teaspoon vanilla.

4. In 3rd hole put 5 tablespoons melted shortening or oil.

5. Mix in 1 cup of cold water. Mix thoroughly.

6. Put in greased and floured pan.

7. Bake in 350° for 30 minutes until done.

Oven Temperature: 350°F

Servings: 12
Yield: 1 square baking dish

Cooking Times
Preparation Time: 15 minutes
Cooking Time: 30 minutes
Total Time: 45 minutes

Zucchini Cake

1/2 cup margarine
1/2 cup vegetable oil
1 3/4 cup sugar
3 large eggs
1 teaspoon vanilla
1/2 cup sour milk (milk mixed with a teaspoon of vinegar)
2 1/2 cups flour
4 tablespoons cocoa powder
1 teaspoon baking soda
1 teaspoon baking powder
1/2 teaspoon cinnamon
1/2 teaspoon cloves
2 cups shredded zucchini

1. Shred zucchini.
2. Cream margarine and vegetable oil.
3. Add sugar, eggs, vanilla and sour milk.
4. Sift flour, cocoa, baking soda, baking powder, cinnamon, cloves.
5. Add to wet mixture.
6. Add shredded zucchini.
7. Mix and spread in baking pan.
8. Bake at 350° for 35 minutes.

Servings: 20

Cooking Times
Preparation Time: 15 minutes
Cooking Time: 35 minutes
Total Time: 50 minutes

Crossing the Three T's of Cooking

Cakes

Cookies

Even though I have been making cookies for a long time, I have decided that when it comes to baking, one should never stop learning. Consequently, I have changed the way I make chocolate chip cookies several times and only save those recipes that are truly awesome. The molasses cookie and gingersnaps come out the same way each time and are a favorite for our cookie boxes at Christmas. The oatmeal cookie is a personal favorite because I like the crispy results. The coconut butterballs are my husband's favorite and my daughter-in-law likes the sugar cookies to decorate at Christmas. The crispy little critters known as cereal cookies were a favorite of my nephew's. Recently, my three-year-old granddaughter was playing her Memory game at my house and matched up the cookie cards and pointed to her mouth indicating that she wanted a cookie. Unfortunately, Grandma didn't have any cookies and she was so disappointed. She would have settled for a store-bought morsel. Speaking of store-bought, my mother used to have an old tin coffee can that the kids had decorated on the outside and that's what she kept her store-bought cookies in for all the gang. When the grandkids visited her, the first thing they did was head straight to that cookie tin for their treat.

Molasses cookies for tea time.

BAKLAVA

1 16-ounce phyllo pastry sheets defrosted according to package directions
1 pound chopped nuts
1 cup butter
1 teaspoon cinnamon

1 cup water
1 cup sugar
1 teaspoon vanilla
1/2 cup honey

1. Preheat oven to 350°. Butter the bottoms and sides of a 9 x 13 inch pan.
2. Chop nuts and toss with cinnamon. Set aside. Unroll phyllo dough. Cut whole stack in half to fit in pan. Cover phyllo with a dampened cloth to keep from drying out as you work. Place two sheets of dough in pan, butter thoroughly. Repeat until you have 8 layers. Sprinkle 2 to 3 tablespoons of nut mixture on top. Top with two sheets of dough, butter, nuts, layering as you go. The top layer should be about 6 to 8 sheets deep.
3. Using a sharp knife cut into diamond or square shapes all the way to the bottom of the pan. You may cut into 4 long rows to make the diagonal cuts. Bake for about 50 minutes until baklava is golden and crisp.
4. Make sauce while baklava is baking. Boil sugar and water until sugar is melted. Add vanilla and honey. Simmer for about 20 minutes.
5. Remove baklava from oven and immediately spoon sauce over it. Let cool. Serve in cupcake papers. This freezes well.

Oven Temperature: 350°F

Servings: 18

Cooking Times
Preparation Time: 30 minutes
Cooking Time: 50 minutes
Total Time: 1 hour and 20 minutes

BROWN SUGAR CHRISTMAS COOKIES

1 cup margarine
1 cup brown sugar
1 cup white sugar
4 eggs
6 cups flour

2 teaspoons vanilla
2 teaspoons baking powder
1 teaspoon salt
2 tablespoons cream or evaporated milk

1. Cream margarine with sugars, add eggs.
2. Blend dry ingredients and mix with sugar mixture.
3. Add milk.
4. Shape cookies or use cookie cutters for desired shapes.
5. Bake at 350° for 15 minutes.

Frosting

3 tablespoons butter
2 1/2 cups confectioner's sugar
2 1/2 tablespoons milk
1 teaspoon vanilla

1. Mix all frosting ingredients with an electric mixer.

Oven Temperature: 350°F

Servings: 35
Yield: 6 dozen

Cooking Times
Preparation Time: 15 minutes
Cooking Time: 15 minutes

BUTTERSCOTCH BROWNIES

1/4 cup shortening
1 cup light brown sugar
1 egg
3/4 cup sifted all purpose flour
1 teaspoon baking powder
1/2 teaspoon salt
1/2 teaspoon vanilla
1/2 cup chopped pecans

1. Heat oven to 350°.
2. Melt shortening over low heat.
3. Remove from heat and blend in brown sugar. Cool.
4. Stir in egg.
5. Stir in flour, baking powder, and salt.
6. Stir in vanilla and pecans.
7. Spread in well greased and floured square pan, 8 x 8 x 2 inches.
8. Bake 25 minutes. Don't over bake.
9. Cut into bars while warm, approximately 18 bars.

Oven Temperature: 350°F

Servings: 18

Cooking Times
Preparation Time: 10 minutes
Cooking Time: 25 minutes
Total Time: 35 minutes

Carol's Peanut Butter Crisscrosses

1 cup shortening
1 cup granulated sugar
1 cup brown sugar
2 eggs
1 teaspoon vanilla

1 cup peanut butter
3 cups flour
2 teaspoons soda
1/2 teaspoon salt

1. Cream shortening, sugars, eggs and vanilla.
2. Stir in peanut butter.
3. Sift dry ingredients.
4. Stir into creamed mixture.
5. Roll cookie dough between hands to form a ball. Dip in granulated sugar. Place on the cookie sheet and use a fork to press dough making crisscross marks on the top of each cookie.
6. Bake at 350° about 10 to 12 minutes until done.

Yield: 5 dozen cookies

Cooking Times
Cooking Time: 10 minutes

CEREAL COOKIES

1/2 cup margarine
1/2 cup white sugar
1/2 cup brown sugar
1 egg
1/2 teaspoon vanilla
1 cup unsifted flour
1/2 teaspoon baking powder

1/2 teaspoon soda
1/4 teaspoon salt
1 cup crispy rice cereal
1/2 cup coconut
1 cup quick cooking oats

1. Cream together margarine and sugars, add egg and vanilla.

2. Sift together flour, soda, baking powder and salt. Add to the above.

3. Add cereal, rolled oats, and coconut.

4. Drop by teaspoons onto cookie sheet.

5. Bake at 375°, about 12 minutes.

Oven Temperature: 375°F

Servings: 12
Yield: 2 dozen

Cooking Times
Preparation Time: 10 minutes
Cooking Time: 12 minutes
Total Time: 22 minutes

COCONUT BUTTERBALLS

1 cup butter or margarine, softened
1/4 cup sifted powdered sugar
1 teaspoon vanilla extract
2 cups all-purpose flour
1 1/2 cups flaked coconut
Sifted powdered sugar

1. Cream butter or margarine until light and fluffy; gradually add sugar and vanilla and mix well. Blend in flour, then coconut. The batter is crumbly until you form it into balls.

2. Roll into 1-inch balls and place on ungreased cookie sheet.

3. Place cookie sheet in refrigerator for about 15 minutes.

4. Bake at 350 degrees F about 15 minutes or until delicately browned. While still warm, roll in powdered sugar.

Oven Temperature: 350°F

Servings: 20
Yield: 4 dozen

Cooking Times
Preparation Time: 10 minutes
Cooking Time: 15 minutes
Inactive Time: 15 minutes

CRISPY OATMEAL COOKIES

3/4 pound (3 sticks) unsalted butter
1 cup light brown sugar
1 1/8 cup granulated sugar
1 large egg
1 1/2 teaspoons vanilla extract
3 cups rolled oats (not instant)
1 1/2 cups all-purpose flour
3/4 teaspoon kosher salt
2 1/2 teaspoons baking soda
1 1/2 cups raisins

1. Preheat the oven to 350 degrees F.
2. In a mixer, cream the butter until fluffy. Add the sugars, and cream together until light and fluffy. Add the egg and vanilla and mix well.
3. In a bowl, stir together the oats, flour, salt, and baking soda. Mixing slowly, add the oat mixture to the butter mixture and mix just until combined. Add raisins and mix just until combined.
4. Drop by tablespoonfuls onto the baking sheets, leaving at least 2-inches between cookies. Bake until browned and crispy around the edges, about 10 to 12 minutes. Start checking at 10 minutes since ovens may vary in temperatures.
5. Let cool on wire racks and store in an airtight container.

Oven Temperature: 350°F

Servings: 15

Cooking Times
Preparation Time: 10 minutes
Cooking Time: 8 minutes
Total Time: 18 minutes

GINGER CRINKLES

2 cups flour	1 teaspoon ginger
1/4 teaspoon salt	3/4 cup shortening
2 teaspoon soda	1 cup brown sugar
1/2 teaspoon cloves	1 egg
1 teaspoon cinnamon	4 tablespoons molasses

1. Cream shortening; add sugar gradually and cream together thoroughly.

2. Beat egg until light; add to creamed mixture and blend well.

3. Add molasses and mix well.

4. Sift flour, salt, soda, cloves, cinnamon and ginger together three times.

5. Shape into balls, the size of walnuts, and dip tops in sugar. Flatten with the bottom of a glass.

6. Place on a greased cookie sheet.

7. Bake in a preheated oven at 350° oven for 12 minutes.

Oven Temperature: 350°F

Servings: 18
Yield: 3 dozen

Cooking Times
Preparation Time: 15 minutes
Cooking Time: 12 minutes
Inactive Time: 1 minute
Total Time: 28 minutes

MOLASSES COOKIES

4 cups all-purpose flour
1/2 teaspoon salt
2 1/4 teaspoons baking soda
2 teaspoons ground ginger
1 1/4 teaspoons ground cloves
1 1/4 teaspoons cinnamon

1 stick (1/2 cup) unsalted butter, softened
1/2 cup vegetable shortening
3 1/2 cups sugar
1/2 cup molasses
2 large eggs

1. Preheat oven to 325°F and lightly grease 2 large baking sheets.

2. In a large bowl whisk together flour, salt, baking soda, ginger, cloves, and cinnamon.

3. In another large bowl with an electric mixer beat together butter, shortening, and 3 cups sugar until light and fluffy and beat in molasses. Beat in eggs, 1 at a time, beating well after each addition. Gradually beat in flour mixture and combine well.

4. In a small shallow bowl put remaining 1/2 cup sugar. Form dough into 2-inch balls and roll in sugar. On baking sheets arrange balls about 4 inches apart and flatten slightly with bottom of a glass dipped in sugar.

5. Bake cookies in batches in middle of the oven 15 minutes, or until puffed and golden. (Cookies should be soft.) Transfer cookies with a metal spatula to racks to cool.

Oven Temperature: 325°F

Servings: 12
Yield: 24
Cooking Times
Preparation Time: 15 minutes
Cooking Time: 15 minutes
Total Time: 30 minutes

NO BAKE COOKIES

2 cups sugar
4 tablespoons cocoa
1/2 cup milk
1/2 cup margarine
1/2 cup peanut butter (creamy)
1 teaspoon vanilla
3 cups oats (quick 1 minute type)

1. Melt margarine and set aside.
2. In a skillet mix sugar and cocoa. Add milk and melted butter. Mix.
3. Heat until the sugar is dissolved.
4. Turn burner off and add peanut butter and blend.
5. Add vanilla and blend. Add oats and mix well.
6. Let stand for 2 to 3 minutes.
7. Drop onto waxed paper and let stand for 1 hour.

Servings: 48

Cooking Times
Preparation Time: 5 minutes
Cooking Time: 6 minutes
Inactive Time: 1 hour
Total Time: 1 hour and 11 minutes

PATTY'S SOUR CREAM COOKIES

    2 cups sugar
    1 cup margarine
    3 eggs
    1 cup sour cream
    1 teaspoon baking soda
    1 teaspoon vanilla
    4 cups flour

1. Cream sugar, margarine, and eggs.
2. Blend in sour cream.
3. Blend flour and baking soda.
4. Mix with creamed mixture, add vanilla. Drop by rounded teaspoon onto a greased cookie sheet.
5. Bake at 350 degrees for 12 to 15 minutes.

Oven Temperature: 350°F

Servings: 36
Yield: 6 dozen

Cooking Times
Preparation Time: 15 minutes

Perfect Chocolate Chip Cookies

1 3/4 cups unbleached all-purpose flour
1/2 teaspoon baking soda
14 tablespoons butter (1 3/4 sticks)
3/4 cup dark brown sugar
1 1/4 cups semisweet chocolate chips
3/4 cups pecan or walnuts toasted

1/2 cup sugar
1 teaspoon salt
2 teaspoons vanilla
1 large egg
1 large egg yolk

1. Whisk baking soda and flour. Set aside.
2. Heat 10 tablespoons butter over medium heat until butter is golden brown about 2 minutes.
3. Transfer to a bowl, add remaining butter.
4. Add both sugars, salt, and vanilla.
5. Add egg and egg yolk, whisk and let stand 3 minutes.
6. Whisk for 30 seconds.
7. Repeat the whisking/resting process two more times.
8. Stir in flour; beat 1 minute.
9. Stir in chips.
10. Divide into 16 portions.
11. Bake at 375° 10 to 14 minutes, centers are still soft, edges golden brown and puffy.
12. Rotate baking sheet halfway through baking.
13. Cool on rack.

Oven Temperature: 375°F

Servings: 16
Yield: 16 huge or 32 cookies

Cooking Times
Preparation Time: 15 minutes
Cooking Time: 8 minutes
Total Time: 23 minutes

PUMPKIN COOKIES

1 1/4 cups white sugar
1/2 cup vegetable oil
1 egg
1/2 teaspoon salt
1/2 teaspoon ground cloves
1 teaspoon cinnamon

1 teaspoon baking soda
2 cups all purpose flour
1 cup pumpkin
1 cup raisins
1/2 cup chopped walnuts

1. Cream sugar and vegetable oil.

2. Add beaten egg.

3. Add pumpkin that has been pureed.

4. Sift flour, baking soda, salt, cloves and cinnamon.

5. Add to creamed mixture.

6. Add raisins and walnuts.

7. Drop cookies onto cookie sheet and bake at 375° for 10 - 13 minutes.

Oven Temperature: 350°F

Servings: 18
Yield: 3 dozen

Cooking Times
Preparation Time: 15 minutes
Cooking Time: 12 minutes
Total Time: 27 minutes

Tips:
You may easily double and triple this recipe for the holidays.

Rum Balls

1 cup vanilla wafers crumbed
1 cup powdered sugar
1 cup finely chopped pecans
2 tablespoons cocoa
1 1/2 tablespoons white corn syrup
1/4 cup rum or 1/4 cup water and
1 teaspoon rum flavoring

1. Combine the crumbs, sugar, pecans, and cocoa.
2. Blend in the corn syrup and rum.
3. Form into balls, using about 2 teaspoons for each ball.
4. Roll in confectioner's sugar.
5. Place in storage container to set completely.

Servings: 14
Yield: 2.5 dozen

Cooking Times
Preparation Time: 20 minutes

Sugar Cookie Dough

3 cups all purpose flour
1/3 cup cornstarch
1 cup butter
1 3-ounce package
  cream cheese, softened

1 teaspoon baking powder
1/2 teaspoon salt
1 egg
1 tablespoon vanilla
3/4 cup sugar

1. In medium mixing bowl, stir together the flour and cornstarch; set aside.

2. In large mixing bowl, beat the butter and cream cheese with an electric mixer on medium to high speed for 30 seconds.

3. Add sugar, baking powder, and salt.

4. Beat in egg and vanilla.

5. Beat in as much of the flour as you can with the mixer. Stir in any remaining flour with a wooden spoon.

6. Roll out dough on floured surface and cut into shapes.

7. Bake in 375° oven 6 to 7 minutes until bottoms are light brown.

8. Cool 1 minute, transfer to wire racks to cool.

9. Frost if desired.

Oven Temperature: 375°F

Servings: 24
Yield: 48 cut out cookies
Cooking Times
Preparation Time: 15 minutes
Cooking Time: 6 minutes
Total Time: 21 minutes

Desserts

Speaking of desserts, I must tell you about the time that I held a Christmas get together for a group of co-workers. Since I could not decide what I wanted to serve for desserts, I settled on a few favorites, only to have the list grow to seven different types of delicacies. Among those selected were rich and creamy Danish Rice Pudding, individual Black Forest Cakes with Cherry filling, Festive Almond Ice Cream Balls, and Special Occasion Glazed Fruit. I had set up a dessert table to showcase my choices and everything was gorgeous. That presented a problem. All of us were having a difficult time deciding what to choose because everything was so tantalizingly tempting. The next day, my husband suggested, no insisted, that I never make that many desserts available at one time again. I truly had to agree with him that it was a little over the top.

Grandma is mentoring again.

BREAD PUDDING WITH LEMON SAUCE

Bread Pudding

5 cups bread, stale bread, stale cake
3 cups warm milk
1/4 teaspoon salt
3 eggs

1/3 cup sugar
1 teaspoon vanilla
1/8 teaspoon nutmeg
1/4 cup raisins

1. Cut bread into slices and trim away crusts if desired. Soak in warm milk for 15 minutes.
2. Beat eggs and add sugar, vanilla, nutmeg, raisins, salt. Pour over soaked bread.
3. Pour bread mixture into a greased baking dish set inside a pan of hot water.
4. Bake at 350° for 45 minutes.

Lemon Sauce

1/4 cup sugar
1 tablespoon cornstarch
1 cup water
2 tablespoons butter

1/2 teaspoon grated lemon peel
1 1/2 tablespoons lemon juice
1/8 teaspoon salt

1. Combine sugar, cornstarch and water and cook over low heat stirring constantly until thickened.
2. In about 5 minutes remove the sauce from the burner and stir in butter, lemon peel, lemon juice and salt. Serve warm over bread pudding.

Oven Temperature: 350°F

Servings: 6

Cooking Times
Preparation Time: 20 minutes
Cooking Time: 45 minutes
Total Time: 1 hour and 5 minutes

Cappuccino Mousse Trifle

- 1 16-ounce frozen prepared pound cake
- 2 1/2 cups cold milk
- 1/3 cup instant coffee granules
- 2 packages instant vanilla pudding mix
- 2 8-ounce containers frozen whipped topping
- 1/4 teaspoon cinnamon
- 1 square semisweet chocolate

1. Cut pound cake into 1 inch squares, set aside.
2. Whisk milk and instant coffee, let stand 5 minutes or until dissolved.
3. Pour 1 cup of milk mixture in another bowl and add pudding, whisk until it begins to thicken.
4. Gently fold in one container of whipped cream.
5. In trifle bowl, assemble 1/3 of cake, 1/3 of coffee milk mixture and 1/3 pudding mixture. Add 1/4 grated chocolate.
6. Repeat layers 2 more times.
7. Spread second container of whipped cream on top. Garnish with chocolate and cinnamon.

Servings: 10

Cooking Times
Preparation Time: 25 minutes

Chocolate-Peanut Butter Pudding

1/2 cup sugar
1/4 cup unsweetened cocoa powder
3 tablespoons cornstarch
2 cups skim milk
1/2 cup peanut butter
1 teaspoon vanilla
1 banana, sliced

1. In a medium saucepan combine the sugar, cocoa powder, and cornstarch.

2. Stir together milk, peanut butter, and vanilla; add to sugar mixture. Cook and stir over medium heat till thickened and bubbly.

3. Cook and stir 2 minutes more. Remove from heat. Pour into a bowl. Cover surface with plastic wrap. Chill till set or up to 24 hours.

4. To serve, spoon half of the pudding into four individual dessert cups; top each using half of the banana. Spoon remaining pudding over bananas; arrange remaining banana slices atop. Serve immediately.

Servings: 4

Cooking Times
Preparation Time: 15 minutes
Inactive Time: 20 hours
Total Time: 20 hours and 15 minutes

Danish Rice Pudding

3 cups cooked rice
2 4-ounce packages instant vanilla pudding mix
1 1/2 cups milk
1 1/4 cups vanilla ice cream, softened
1/2 teaspoon cinnamon
2 cups frozen whipped topping

1. Rinse rice with cold water, drain well.

2. Combine pudding mix, milk, ice cream and cinnamon in mixer bowl. Beat for 1 minute.

3. Fold in rice. Chill until serving time. Fold in whipped topping.

4. Spoon into serving dishes.

Servings: 12

Cooking Times
Preparation Time: 10 minutes
Inactive Time: 2 hours
Total Time: 2 hours and 10 minutes

Festive Almond Ice Cream Balls

2 cups sliced almonds
1 1/2 quarts vanilla ice cream
2 12-ounce packages unsweetened frozen raspberries OR strawberries (2 cups)
1/4 cup sugar
2 tablespoon cherry liqueur
6 mint sprigs, for garnish

1. Preheat oven to 350°.
2. Toast almonds in single layer on baking sheet for 5 minutes or until golden brown, stirring occasionally. Cool.
3. Shape ice cream into 6 large or 12 to 18 small balls, roll in toasted almonds. Freeze until firm.
4. Puree thawed raspberries in blender or food processor container, strain. Add sugar and liqueur; blend well.
5. Spoon raspberry sauce onto dessert plates. Place ice cream ball on each plate.
6. Garnish with mint sprigs.

Oven Temperature: 350°F

Servings: 6

Cooking Times
Preparation Time: 20 minutes
Cooking Time: 5 minutes
Total Time: 25 minutes

GLORIFIED RICE

1 cup rice cooked
1/3 cup sugar
1 12-ounce can of crushed pineapple
1/2 teaspoon vanilla
1/3 cup miniature marshmallows
2 tablespoons maraschino cherries
1 cup whipped cream

1. Mix rice, sugar, pineapple and vanilla.

2. Stir in marshmallows and cherries.

3. Fold in whipped cream.

Servings: 6
Yield: 6 cups

Cooking Times
Preparation Time: 10 minutes
Total Time: 10 minutes

LIME GELATIN DESSERT

1 3-ounce package lime gelatin
1 cup miniature marshmallows
1 3-ounce package cream cheese
1 20-ounce can crushed pineapple drained thoroughly
2 tablespoons really good mayonnaise
1/2 cup chopped pecans

1. Combine gelatin and hot water, and then mix in marshmallows.

2. Add cream cheese and mayonnaise.

3. Beat thoroughly; add crushed pineapple and chopped pecans.

4. Place in a square baking pan. Refrigerate until set.

Servings: 12
Yield: 1 square baking dish
Cooking Times
Preparation Time: 15 minutes
Inactive Time: 1 hour
Total Time: 1 hour and 15 minutes

Tips:
Recipe may be doubled for a 13 x 9 x 2 in pan.

LIMONCELLO CHEESECAKE SQUARES

Nonstick cooking spray
8 ounce purchased biscotti or sugar cookies
6 tablespoons (3/4 stick) unsalted butter, melted
3 tablespoons grated lemon zest
1 12-ounce container fresh whole milk ricotta, drained, at room temperature
2 8-ounce packages cream cheese, at room temperature
1 1/4 cups sugar
1/2 cup Limoncello liqueur, store bought or homemade.
2 teaspoons vanilla extract
4 large eggs, at room temperature

1. Preheat the oven to 350 degrees F. Spray the bottom of a 9 by 9 by 2-inch baking pan with nonstick cooking spray.
2. Finely grind the biscotti in a food processor. Add the melted butter and 1 tablespoon of lemon zest, and process until the crumbs are moistened. Press the crumb mixture over the bottom (not the sides) of the prepared pan.
3. Bake until the crust is golden, about 15 minutes. Cool the crust completely on a cooling rack.
4. Blend the ricotta, cream cheese, and sugar in the food processor until smooth. Blend in the Limoncello, vanilla, and remaining 2 tablespoons of lemon zest.
5. Add the eggs one at a time, and pulse just until blended. Scrape down the sides of the bowl as needed.
6. Pour the cheese mixture over the crust in the pan. Place the baking pan in a large roasting pan with enough hot water to come halfway up the sides of the baking pan.
7. Bake until the cheesecake is golden about 1 hour.
8. Transfer the cake to a rack; cool 1 hour. Refrigerate at least 8 hours. Cut the cake into squares and serve.

Oven Temperature: 350°F

Servings: 12

Cooking Times
Preparation Time: 20 minutes
Cooking Time: 1 hour and 15 minutes
Inactive Time: 10 hours
Total Time: 11 hours and 35 minutes

OLD FASHIONED STAINED GLASS CAKE

12 graham crackers
3/4 cup sugar (1/4 cup for crust, 1/2 for cream)
5 tablespoons unsalted butter melted
3 3-ounce boxes of gelatin (2 red, 1 blue or 2 red and 1 green)
4 1/2 cups boiling water
3/4 cup pineapple juice
1 envelope unflavored gelatin
2 cups heavy (whipping) cream
1 teaspoon vanilla
1/8 teaspoon salt

1. Prepare crust by mixing 1/4 cup sugar with graham cracker crumbs and melted butter. Press the mixture into a spring form pan. Bake at 325° for 12 to 15 minutes. Let cool.
2. Prepare the gelatin filling by mixing 3 separate colors of gelatin in 3 separate pans. Use 1 1/2 cups of boiling water for each color.
3. Let gelatin set for 4 hours. Cut into cubes. Keep chilled until ready to assemble.
4. Make cream filling by mixing 1/4 cup pineapple juice with unflavored gelatin. Let the gelatin set for 1 to 3 minutes.
5. Whisk in remaining pineapple juice, whipped cream, vanilla, salt and remaining sugar for 3 minutes. Reduce speed. Slowly add creamed filling mixture to gelatin mixture. Gently fold in gelatin cubes.
6. Refrigerate for 4 hours. Undo springform pan and cut into slices to serve.

Oven Temperature: 325°F

Servings: 10

Cooking Times
Preparation Time: 25 minutes
Cooking Time: 15 minutes
Inactive Time: 4 hours

Raspberry Walnut Torte

1 1/2 cups walnut pieces
3 tablespoons flour
1 tablespoon baking powder
6 eggs
1 1/4 cups sugar

1 cup whipped cream
2 tablespoons sugar
1/3 cup raspberry preserves
2 cups fresh raspberries

1. Grease and lightly flour pan.
2. Combine nuts, flour, and baking powder.
3. In a blender combine the eggs and sugar. Add in nut mixture and blend.
4. Transfer to prepared pan.
5. Bake in 350° oven for 30 to 35 minutes or until toothpick inserted in center comes out clean.
6. Cool for 10 minutes. Remove from pan.
7. Combine whipping cream and 2 tablespoons of sugar and beat until soft peaks form. Set aside.
8. Heat preserves in a small saucepan or microwave.

To assemble torte, use a serrated knife to cut cake in half.

1. Cut cake in half. Cut each half into 2 layers so you have 4- 8 x 4 inch layers.
2. Transfer 1 layer to the serving plate and evenly spread with 1/4 of the whipped cream.
3. Spread with 1/2 cup of raspberries with about 2 tablespoons of the drizzled preserves.
4. Repeat layers 2 more times, top with final layer.
5. Spread half of the remaining whipped cream over top of cake. To serve, slice with a table knife.

Servings: 8
Yield: 9 x 9 x 2 inch loaf

Cooking Times
Preparation Time: 20 minutes
Cooking Time: 30 minutes
Inactive Time: 4 hours and 20 minutes

RHUBARB COBBLER

Rhubarb Filling

6 cups sliced rhubarb, (1 inch pieces) fresh
1 cup sugar
1/4 cup water
4 teaspoons cornstarch

1. Make filling by mixing rhubarb, sugar, water and cornstarch and letting stand 10 minutes.
2. Cook and stir till thickened and bubbly. Keep hot.

Cobbler

1 cup flour
1/4 cup sugar
1 teaspoon baking powder
1/2 teaspoon cinnamon

3 tablespoons butter
1 egg, beaten
3 tablespoons milk

1. For cobbler, mix flour, sugar, baking powder, and cinnamon.
2. Cut in butter till mixture resembles coarse crumbs. Combine egg and milk. Add to flour mixture stirring just until moistened.
3. Transfer filling to an 8 x 8 x 2 inch baking dish.
4. Drop cobbler into 6 mounds on top of hot filling.
5. Bake in a 400° oven 20 to 25 minutes or till a toothpick inserted into topping comes out clean.
6. Serve warm with ice cream if desired.

Oven Temperature: 400°F

Servings: 6

Cooking Times
Preparation Time: 10 minutes
Cooking Time: 25 minutes
Total Time: 35 minutes

Special Occasion Glazed Fruit

1 16-ounce pineapple chunks, drained (reserve juice)
1 11-ounce mandarin oranges, drained (reserve juice)
1 small vanilla instant pudding mix
1/4 cup orange instant breakfast drink
1 20-ounce cherry pie filling
2 tablespoons poppy seeds
2 or 3 bananas, sliced

1. Drain pineapple and oranges, reserving juices.
2. Combine reserved juices, instant pudding mix and instant breakfast drink mix in bowl; mix well.
3. Add pineapple, oranges, pie filling and poppy seed.
4. Chill overnight.
5. Stir in bananas gently just before serving.

Servings: 8

Cooking Times
Preparation Time: 15 minutes
Inactive Time: 8 hours and 20 minutes
Total Time: 8 hours and 35 minutes

Crossing the Three T's of Cooking

Desserts

Eggs, Cheese, Legumes

Well, I grew up on a farm and farmers typically didn't get to eat dinner or supper as we would say, until late evening after the chores were done. Therefore, it was not unusual to get off the school bus in the afternoon and enjoy a snack of scrambled eggs or an egg sandwich with really good mayonnaise to tide us over until the evening meal. Consequently, I still enjoy a good egg sandwich and even add a slice of cheese. The egg casserole is prepared the night before making it a great Christmas morning breakfast. The farmhouse where I grew up had a wood cook stove in the kitchen and every Saturday morning my dad would start a pot of beans for his infamous bean soup. My mother's contribution was always asking him if he had seasoned the soup yet. I often felt he left it up to her discretion because she had such a knack for throwing in various spices and seasonings that resulted in a savory concoction.

Egg Casserole

EGG CASSEROLE

12 eggs
Salt and freshly ground black pepper
3 tablespoons parsley flakes
1 teaspoon nutmeg
12 slices bacon
1 cup sour cream
1 cup cheddar cheese grated

1. Brown bacon.

2. Beat eggs.

3. Mix in salt, pepper, parsley, nutmeg.

4. Scramble to a just moistened stage.

5. Spread in baking dish.

6. Top with crumbled bacon, sour cream and grated cheese.

7. Refrigerate overnight.

8. Bake at 350° for 35 minutes.

Oven Temperature: 350°F

Servings: 8

Cooking Times
Preparation Time: 20 minutes
Cooking Time: 35 minutes
Total Time: 55 minutes

Tips:
May use sausage or ham for meat.

Morning Pecan Casserole

1 8-ounce package brown and serve sausage patties
1 16-ounce loaf of raisin bread, cubed
6 eggs
1 1/2 cups milk
1 1/2 cups half and half cream
1 teaspoon vanilla
1/4 teaspoon nutmeg
1/4 teaspoon cinnamon
1 cup brown sugar
1 cup chopped pecans
1/2 cup butter
2 tablespoons maple syrup

1. Brown patties on both sides; cut into bite size pieces.
2. Spray baking dish (3 qt); Put in bread cubes, sausage pieces.
3. Beat eggs, milk, half and half, vanilla, nutmeg, and cinnamon.
4. Pour over sausage, cover and refrigerate 8 hours or overnight.
5. Prepare topping by mixing brown sugar, pecans, butter and syrup.
6. Drop by teaspoons over egg mixture.
7. Bake at 350° 35 to 40 minutes.

Oven Temperature: 350°F

Servings: 8

Cooking Times
Preparation Time: 15 minutes
Cooking Time: 35 minutes
Inactive Time: 9 hours
Total Time: 9 hours and 50 minutes

Tips:
May bake in custard cups, if so bake them for 25 to 30 minutes.

Swiss Cheese and Mushroom Quiche

1 9-inch deep dish frozen pie shell
1 1/2 cups Swiss cheese grated
1 medium onion chopped
1/4 pound mushrooms (chopped fine)
2 tablespoons butter
Basil
Salt and freshly ground black pepper
4 eggs
1 1/2 cups milk
3 tablespoons flour
1/4 teaspoon salt
1/4 teaspoon dry mustard
Paprika

1. Cover the bottom of the pie crust with 1 1/2 cups grated Swiss cheese.
2. Cover cheese with the onion and mushrooms that have been sautéed in butter with salt and pepper and basil.
3. Make custard by beating the eggs together with milk, flour, salt and dry mustard.
4. Pour custard over the mushroom layer.
5. Sprinkle with paprika.
6. Bake at 375° for 40 to 45 minutes or until the center is solid when jiggled.

Oven Temperature: 375°F

Servings: 6
Yield: 1 pie

Cooking Times
Preparation Time: 15 minutes
Cooking Time: 40 minutes
Total Time: 55 minutes

Tips:

You may use gruyere cheese or cheddar cheese instead of Swiss cheese.

Use fresh tomato slices instead of mushrooms. (Note: tomatoes would not need to be sautéed first).

Add 1 teaspoon prepared horseradish.

Fish & Shellfish

My mother used to make salmon patties (many times she used canned mackerel) for the family because it seemed to stretch the food budget. Because I grew up in such a large family, I learned how to make the most of each cut of meat and learned to be creative with leftovers. Throughout my childhood stories were told of how my parents invited strangers to help work in the fields and then prepared dinner for them. Even though there were already enough mouths to feed with a large family, it was nothing to share with those who needed a meal. Several times, my mother's brother would have no where to stay and would spend a couple of days with my folks. His gratefulness was always evident when he would finish eating and turn to my mother and say, "Margaret, you can make a meal out of anything!" So that was the concept and training that I received from my mother... use what you have. I can vividly remember only one time that I actually had to throw a dish out because I used sweetened condensed milk instead of condensed milk. The resulting main dish was sweet instead of savory. Consequently, I never made that mistake again. Try the fish casserole with your favorite fish such as cod or tilapia. My husband's specialty is the Smoked Salmon which I absolutely adore. His leftover Smoked Salmon is great in omelets, bagel and cream cheese and yes, it even makes stellar salmon patties.

Fish Casserole

BRINE FOR SMOKED SALMON

1 bottle chardonnay
1/2 cup kosher salt
1 cup white sugar
3/4 cup brown sugar
Lemon pepper to taste
Freshly ground black pepper to taste
4 cloves garlic, crushed or to taste
  or 1 tablespoon of garlic powder
1 dash hot pepper sauce (optional)
2 lemons, sliced and crushed
2 oranges, sliced and crushed
1 lime, sliced and crushed
1 large yellow onion, sliced
1/8 cup maple syrup

1. Pour the chardonnay into a pan for brining. If you must use a pot, use one that does not contain aluminum.

2. Stir in the kosher salt, white sugar, brown sugar, lemon pepper, parsley, and ground black pepper.

3. Add the garlic, hot pepper sauce, lemons, oranges, lime and onion.

4. Soak your salmon in this brine for 12 to 36 hours.

5. Smoke using your desired method.

Servings: 24

Cooking Times
Preparation Time: 1 hour and 10 minutes

COD CAKES

1 pound cod fillets or imitation flake crabmeat
1 cup coarsely crushed round buttery crackers
2 eggs
1/4 cup milk
1/4 cup chopped parsley
2 teaspoons Worcestershire sauce
1 teaspoon dried dill weed
1/2 teaspoon salt
1/4 teaspoon pepper

1. In a medium bowl, mix cod, cracker crumbs, eggs, milk, parsley, Worcestershire sauce, dill weed, salt, and pepper until well blended.

2. Using about 1/4 cup of the mixture at a time, shape into eight 3-inch patties.

3. Into a large skillet, pour oil to a depth of 1/4 inch; place over medium heat.

4. When hot, add cod cakes and cook for 5 minutes on each side or until well browned.

5. Remove from skillet and drain on paper towels.

6. Serve hot or cold.

Servings: 4

Cooking Times
Preparation Time: 5 minutes
Cooking Time: 10 minutes
Total Time: 15 minutes

FISH CASSEROLE

6 cod fish
Salt and pepper to taste
1 bag frozen potatoes
1 10-ounce cream of celery soup
1/4 cup milk
2 tablespoons really good mayonnaise
3 ounce cheddar cheese grated

1. Place fish in bottom of baking dish.

2. Sprinkle with salt and pepper.

3. Spread potatoes over top of fish.

4. Mix soup, milk and salad dressing and pour over top.

5. Add shredded cheese.

6. Bake for 30 to 40 minutes at 350°.

Oven Temperature: 350°F

Servings: 6

Cooking Times
Preparation Time: 15 minutes
Cooking Time: 35 minutes
Total Time: 50 minutes

Goldfish (Salmon) Cakes

- 1 15-ounce can pink salmon
- 2 tablespoons mayonnaise
- 2 tablespoons chopped parsley
- 1 tablespoon lemon juice
- 1 teaspoon Worcestershire sauce
- 1/2 teaspoon black pepper
- 1 large egg
- 1/2 package unseasoned bread crumbs
- 2 tablespoons vegetable oil

1. In medium size bowl, combine salmon, mayonnaise, parsley, lemon juice, Worcestershire sauce, and pepper.
2. In small bowl, beat egg. Spread bread crumbs on a sheet of waxed paper.
3. Shape salmon mixture into 4 round, flattened cakes. Dip each into beaten egg then coat with bread crumbs.
4. Place on plate; cover and refrigerate 30 minutes.
5. In large skillet, heat 2 tablespoons oil. Fry salmon cakes, turning once, until golden brown and heated through 3 to 5 minutes on each side. Add remaining oil to skillet if needed.
6. Serve with tartar sauce.

Servings: 4

Cooking Times
Preparation Time: 5 minutes
Cooking Time: 5 minutes
Inactive Time: 30 minutes

Crossing the Three T's of Cooking

Meat

One of the advantages of growing up on a dairy farm was we usually had an abundance of milk and beef. Additionally, my mother raised chickens so we had chicken and eggs as well. Our meals were rounded out with fresh vegetables from the garden. On Sundays, my mother would prepare a huge meal and whoever happened to drop in was welcome to stay for dinner. Her favorite process was to throw in a beef roast alongside a ham roast in a huge roasting pan. Sounds crazy but it was good. When she made meatloaf, she typically pressed it into a large roasting pan instead of forming loaves. We often enjoyed leftover meatloaf sandwiches with butter and mayonnaise. Try my recipe for meatloaf ...even the pickiest eaters seem to like this version. Pictured is my husband's grilled meatloaf using my recipe. Yes, we still look forward to meatloaf sandwiches.

Meatloaf off the grill.

BAKED BEEF STROGANOFF

3 pounds round steak cut in strips
1 cup dry red wine
1 envelope dry onion soup mix
2 8-ounce cans sliced mushrooms
1 10-ounce can cream of chicken soup
1 10-ounce can cream of celery soup
1 10-ounce can cream of mushroom soup
1 teaspoon salt
1/2 teaspoon pepper
2 cups sour cream
Crunchy Christmas Rice

1. Preheat oven to 300°. Cut round steak into strips or cubes.
2. Combine steak with wine, dry soup mix, mushrooms, canned soups and pepper in roasting pan, mix well.
3. Bake for 3 to 4 hours or until steak is very tender. Stir in sour cream just before serving.
4. Serve over Crunchy Christmas Rice or noodles if desired.

Oven Temperature: 300°F

Servings: 8

Cooking Times
Preparation Time: 20 minutes
Cooking Time: 3 hours
Total Time: 3 hours and 20 minutes

Barbecue Ribs in Slow Cooker

   Canola oil or vegetable oil
   2 small red onions, finely chopped
   3-4 cloves garlic, peeled and minced
   1 lemon, juiced
   1 cup brown sugar, packed
   1/2 cup cider vinegar
   1 cup ketchup
   2 tablespoons Worcestershire sauce
   1 tablespoon hot pepper sauce, or to taste
   1/2 teaspoon chili powder
   3 racks of baby back ribs cut into 3-4 rib pieces

1. In a skillet placed on stove top set to medium heat, add oil and cook onions and garlic until softened and lightly browned.

2. Stir in remaining ingredients and simmer gently for about 5 minutes.

3. Remove half the sauce to use for serving.

4. Add ribs to sauce to slow cooker, cover, and cook on Low for 7-9 hours or on High for 4-6 hours.

5. To serve, cut ribs between bones and pass extra sauce.

Servings: 6
Yield: 6-7 quarts

Cooking Times
Preparation Time: 5 minutes
Cooking Time: 7 hours
Total Time: 7 hours and 5 minutes

Betty's Polish Sausage and Sauerkraut

3 pounds sauerkraut, rinsed and squeezed dry
2 1/2 pounds polish sausage
1 cup sugar
1/2 quart tomato juice
2 1/2 ounces ketchup
Salt and pepper to taste

1. Slice polish sausage.

2. Drain sauerkraut in colander, let stand 30 minutes or more.

3. In separate bowl, mix tomato juice, ketchup, sugar, and salt and pepper to taste.

4. Put drained sauerkraut, sausage, and sauce in roaster or crock pot.

5. Cook for 5 to 8 hours.

Servings: 12

Cooking Times
Preparation Time: 20 minutes
Cooking Time: 5 minutes
Total Time: 25 minutes

Tips:
You may double and triple the recipe.
The longer it cooks, the better it tastes.

BRAISED BEEF SHORT RIBS

4 pounds beef short ribs
3 tablespoons vegetable oil
Kosher salt
Black pepper
3/4 cups onions, chopped
1/2 cup celery chopped
1/2 cup carrots peeled and diced
1 teaspoon paprika
2 tablespoons rosemary
1 tablespoon garlic clove, minced
Red wine for deglazing
3 cups liquid for braising (combination of red wine, broth, soy sauce, (1/4 cup) beer)

Oven Temperature: 325°F

Servings: 8

Cooking Times
Preparation Time: 25 minutes
Cooking Time: 3 hours
Inactive Time: 10 minutes
Total Time: 3 hours and 35 minutes

Continued on next page

Braised Beef Short Ribs

1. Heat oven to 325°.

2. In an 8-quart Dutch oven, heat 2 tablespoons of oil over medium heat.

3. Season the ribs with 2 teaspoons salt and 1 teaspoon pepper.

4. Cook ribs on both sides until browned, about 3 to 4 minutes per side.

5. Transfer the ribs to a platter. Pour off all but a thin layer of fat from the pan.

6. Deglaze the pot with your choice of deglazing liquid (wine, beer, apple cider, sherry etc).

7. Add the remaining 1 tablespoon of oil and your choice of aromatics (onions, leeks, carrots, celery, and fennel).

8. Add the spices, herbs.

9. Transfer the ribs back to the pot and cover with the braising liquid (you may use broth, red or white wine, beer, tomatoes, soy sauce etc.).

10. Bring the liquid to a simmer, cover and put the pot in the oven.

11. Cook turning the ribs with tongs every 40 minutes until they are fork tender (about 2 3/4 hours).

12. Transfer the ribs to a serving dish, and let sauce sit in pan to cool. Skim off as much of the fat as possible.

13. Serve with garlic mashed potatoes.

ENCHILADAS

Mexican Sauce

3 tablespoons olive oil
2 medium onions coarsely chopped
1 clove garlic clove, chopped
2 medium tomatoes, diced
1 1/2 cups beef bouillon stock made with 2 teaspoons bouillon granules or 2 beef bouillon cubes and 1 ½ cups of water
1/2 teaspoon hot sauce
1/4 teaspoon salt
2 teaspoons chili powder

1. Heat oil in skillet. Add onion, garlic, cook until tender.
2. Add tomatoes, stock, and hot sauce, stir in salt and chili powder. Bring to boil, simmer 30 minutes.

Servings: 6
Yield: 12 tortillas

Cooking Times
Preparation Time: 30 minutes
Cooking Time: 10 minutes
Total Time: 40 minutes

Continued on next page

Enchiladas

Tortillas

1/4 teaspoon hot sauce
1 cup milk
3/4 cup cornstarch
2 eggs
1/3 cup cornmeal
1/2 teaspoon salt
2 tablespoons melted butter

1. Add Tabasco to milk. Add to cornstarch and stir to a smooth paste.
2. Beat eggs; add cornmeal, salt and cornstarch mixture. Stir in butter. Use 3 tablespoons of mixture for each tortilla. Quickly pour into lightly greased heated 7-inch skillet. Brown on one side; turn to brown on other side.

Filling

1 cup diced cooked chicken or 1 cup ground beef, cooked and drained
1 1/2 cups cheddar cheese shredded

To make enchiladas, drop one tortilla quickly into heated Mexican sauce to soften.

1. Put 2 tablespoons of the filling in center of each tortilla. Roll up and place seam side down in shallow baking dish. Pour sauce over all.
2. Bake at 350° oven for 10 minutes. Sprinkle with any remaining ingredients.

Filet Mignons with Mushroom Madeira Sauce

1/2 pound fresh mushrooms (stems removed), sliced (about 2 ½ cups)
1 tablespoon olive oil
2 cloves garlic clove, minced
1 teaspoon thyme
1/2 teaspoon freshly ground black pepper
4 beef tenderloin (fillet), thinly sliced

2 shallots, chopped
2 cloves garlic, finely minced
1 cup Madeira
1/2 cup beef broth
1/4 cup whipping cream

1. Remove stems from mushrooms, discarding stems. Cut mushroom caps into thin slices.

2. Combine oil and next 3 ingredients; coat steaks with mixture. Place a large nonstick skillet over medium high heat until hot; add steaks, and cook 4 minutes a side, turning once. Remove steaks from skillet, reserving drippings in skillet. Keep steaks warm.

3. Cook shallot and garlic in drippings, stirring constantly, until tender. Add Madeira; bring to a boil.

4. Reduce heat, and simmer 10 minutes or until reduced to 1/2 cup.

5. Add broth and mushrooms; cook 3 minutes or until tender, stirring often. Remove from heat. Stir in whipping cream; spoon some of the sauce onto serving plates, and add steaks. Garnish if desired. Serve hot.

Servings: 4

Cooking Times
Preparation Time: 7 minutes
Cooking Time: 21 minutes
Total Time: 28 minutes

NEW YORK STYLE REUBEN SANDWICH

8 slices rye bread
4 teaspoons coarse grain mustard
1 pound corned beef, sliced thin
1/2 pound Swiss cheese
8 ounces sauerkraut, drained
1/2 cup Russian Salad Dressing (See Russian Dressing recipe)
1/2 tablespoon butter

1. Prepare the sandwiches. Place 4 slices rye bread and spread each slice with 1 teaspoon mustard.

2. Layer each bread slice with 1/4 pound of corned beef followed by 2 ounces Swiss cheese and 2 ounces of sauerkraut. Spread 2 tablespoons of Russian Salad Dressing on the remaining 4 slices and place dressing side down on top of sauerkraut.

3. Toast the sandwiches: In a large nonstick skillet, melt butter over medium heat. When the butter begins to sizzle, place the sandwiches in the pan and toast until golden brown, about 3 to 5 minutes.

4. Turn sandwiches over and continue to toast for 3 to 5 minutes more.

5. Serve immediately.

Servings: 4

Cooking Times
Preparation Time: 10 minutes
Cooking Time: 10 minutes
Total Time: 20 minutes

OUT TO THE FARM STEAK WITH BISCUITS AND GRAVY

Steak and Gravy

1 1/2 cups, plus 2 tablespoons all-purpose flour
1/2 teaspoon freshly ground black pepper
8 4-ounce cube steaks
1 teaspoon all purpose seasoning salt
2 cups buttermilk
2/3 cup vegetable oil
1 1/2 teaspoons salt
1 quart whole milk
1/4 teaspoon grated fresh nutmeg
1 bunch green onions, or 1 medium yellow onion, sliced

Oven Temperature: 400°F

Servings: 4

Cooking Times
Preparation Time: 20 minutes
Cooking Time: 1 hour
Total Time: 1 hour and 20 minutes

Continued on next page

Out to the Farm Steak with Biscuits and Gravy

1. Combine 1 1/2 cups flour and 1/4 teaspoon of pepper in a small bowl. Sprinkle meat with the all purpose seasoning salt, and then dredge the meat in buttermilk and then flour. Heat 1/2 cup oil in a heavy skillet over medium-high heat. Add 2 or 4 of the steaks to the hot oil and fry until browned, about 5 to 6 minutes per side. Remove each steak to a paper towel-lined plate to drain. Repeat with the remaining steaks, adding up to 1/4 cup more oil, as needed.

2. Make the gravy by adding the 2 tablespoons remaining flour to the pan drippings, scraping the bottom with a wooden spoon. Stir in the remaining 1/4 teaspoon pepper, and the salt. Reduce the heat to medium and cook, stirring frequently, until the flour is medium brown and the mixture is bubbly. Slowly add the whole milk and the all purpose seasoning, stirring constantly. Return the steaks to the skillet and bring to a boil over medium-high heat. Reduce the heat to low, and place the onions on top of the steaks. Cover the pan, and let simmer for 30 minutes.

Basic Biscuits (makes a lot)

1 package yeast
1/2 cup lukewarm water
5 cups all-purpose flour
1 teaspoon baking soda
1/2 teaspoon salt
1 tablespoon baking powder
2 tablespoons sugar
3/4 cup solid shortening
2 cups buttermilk

1. Preheat oven to 400 degrees F. Dissolve yeast in warm water; set aside. Mix dry ingredients together. Cut in shortening. Add yeast and buttermilk and mix well. Turn dough onto lightly floured surface and roll out to desired thickness. Cut with small biscuit cutter and place on greased baking sheet. Bake for 12 minutes or until golden brown.

2. Split biscuits in half and top with fried steak and drizzle with gravy.

PEPPER STEAK

2 pounds round steak cut in strips
2 tablespoons oil
1/4 teaspoon ground ginger
1 15-ounce can tomatoes, undrained
2 large green peppers, sliced
1/2 cup cold water
1 tablespoon cornstarch
Cooked rice

1/4 cup soy sauce
1 sliced onion
1 clove garlic minced
1 teaspoon sugar
1/2 teaspoon salt
1/4 teaspoon pepper

1. Brown beef in the oil.
2. Combine beef, soy sauce, onion, garlic, sugar, salt, pepper, and ginger in slow cooker. Cover; cook on low for 5-6 hours. Stir in tomatoes and peppers; cook for one more hour.
3. Combine cornstarch and water; stir into slow cooker.
4. Turn heat to high and cook for 20-30 minutes or until sauce is thickened.
5. Serve over rice.

Servings: 6

Cooking Times
Total Time: 5 minutes

PORK WITH RED PLUM SAUCE

1 4-pound rolled boneless pork loin roast
1 10-ounce jar red plum preserves
1/2 cup firmly packed brown sugar
1/4 cup soy sauce
2 tablespoons lemon juice
2 teaspoons prepared mustard
3 drops hot sauce
1/4 teaspoon onion salt
1/4 teaspoon garlic salt
1 cup water
3/4 cup chopped onion
2 tablespoons butter
1/3 cup chili sauce

1. Sprinkle roast with onion and garlic salts.
2. Place roast on a rack in a roasting pan, add water to pan. Cover with aluminum foil, bake at 325° for 2 hours.
3. Cook onion in butter in a medium saucepan over medium high heat, stirring constantly.
4. Add plum preserves and remaining 6 ingredients.
5. Cook over medium heat uncovered for 15 minutes, stirring often.
6. Pour half of sauce over roast.
7. Bake, uncovered, 20 more minutes, or until a meat thermometer inserted in thickest part of roast registers 160°, basting with half of remaining sauce.
8. Transfer roast to a serving platter. Let stand 10 minutes before slicing.
9. Serve sauce with roast.

Oven Temperature: 325°F

Servings: 12

Cooking Times
Preparation Time: 15 minutes
Cooking Time: 2 hours and 20 minutes
Total Time: 2 hours and 35 minutes

Reuben Casserole

8 to 10 slices seeded rye bread
Softened butter
1 large chopped onion, divided
1/2 pound ground pork
2 pounds sauerkraut, rinsed and squeezed dry
1 cup mushrooms, chopped
1 1/2 cups sour cream
1 tablespoon prepared mustard
3/4 cup whole milk
1 tablespoon flour
1 cup or more chicken stock
8 ounces medium egg noodles, parboiled and drained
1 1/2 pounds fresh white Polish sausage, cooked, casing removed and cut into 1/2-inch pieces
2 tablespoons melted butter
1 1/2 cups grated Swiss cheese

Oven Temperature: 350°F

Cooking Times
Preparation Time: 30 minutes
Cooking Time: 35 minutes
Total Time: 1 hour and 5 minutes

Continued on next page

Reuben Casserole

Salt and pepper

1. Remove crusts from rye bread. Shred crusts to make crumbs and set aside. Remove crusts from the bread slices and butter. Place buttered side down in the bottom of a large casserole dish (larger than 9x13 inches).

2. In a medium skillet, sauté 1/2 the chopped onion with ground pork until onions are light brown. Transfer the drippings and all, to sauerkraut and mix.

3. In the same skillet, without rinsing, add 2 tablespoons butter, remaining onions and chopped mushrooms, and sauté until onions are translucent.

4. In a medium saucepan, combine sour cream, mustard, milk and flour. Heat over low, stirring constantly, until it thickens. Add the stock and stir until it thickens but still can be poured. Add more stock, if necessary to achieve the right consistency. Add the mushroom-onion mixture, combining well.

5. Heat oven to 350 degrees. To assemble the casserole, spread the sauerkraut mixture over the bread in the casserole dish. Spread noodles over sauerkraut and pour the sauce over the noodles. Cover with a layer of sausage.

6. Mix 2 tablespoons melted butter with rye bread crumbs and sprinkle over top of casserole. Cover tightly with foil and bake for 35 minutes.

7. Remove foil and scatter cheese over the top of the casserole and bake another 10 minutes or until cheese is melted and bubbly. Let casserole sit for at least 5 minutes before serving.

Salisbury Steak with Mashed Potatoes

1 pound medium sized potatoes peeled and quartered
1 1/4 pound ground beef chuck
1/2 cup fresh bread crumbs
1/2 cup finely chopped onion
1/4 pound fresh mushrooms, sliced
1 1/2 cups water
3 tablespoons flour
1 large egg
1 1/2 teaspoons salt
1/4 teaspoon pepper
1/8 teaspoon ground allspice
1/2 cup milk, warmed
1 tablespoon butter
1 tablespoon olive oil
1 tablespoon ketchup

1. In 2-quart saucepan, heat 3 inches water to boiling. Add potatoes; return to boiling.
2. Cook, uncovered, until tender 20 to 25 minutes. Drain very well.
3. Shake potatoes in saucepan over low heat to dry. Remove from heat.
4. Meanwhile, in medium-sized bowl, combine ground chuck, breadcrumbs, onions, egg, 1/2 teaspoon salt, pepper and the allspice. Shape mixture into 4 oval patties and set aside.
5. With potato masher or electric mixer, mash potatoes. Gradually beat in milk. Add butter and 1/2 teaspoon salt. Beat until fluffy. Keep warm until ready to serve.
6. In 10-inch skillet, heat oil. Sauté beef patties, turning until well browned and cooked through 3 to 5 minutes on each side. Remove steaks to serving plates and keep warm.
7. Add mushrooms to skillet. Sauté until golden. In small bowl, gradually beat water into flour. Stir into mushroom mixture along with ketchup and remaining salt and pepper. Cook, stirring to remove browned on bits until gravy has thickened. Spoon some of the gravy over steaks. Serve with mashed potatoes.

Servings: 4

Cooking Times

Preparation Time: 15 minutes
Cooking Time: 25 minutes
Total Time: 40 minutes

SLOPPY JOES

5 bacon slices
1 1/2 pounds ground beef
1 onion finely chopped
4 garlic cloves, minced
1 carrot minced
3 tablespoons tomato paste
1/2 cup ketchup

2 tablespoons red wine vinegar
2 tablespoons soy sauce
1 tablespoon sugar
2 bay leaves
1 pinch chili flakes
Salt and pepper to taste

1. Heat a heavy skillet over high heat. Add the bacon slices and cook until some of the fat renders and the strips are crisp.
2. Remove from the pan and set aside.
3. Add the ground beef and brown, stirring and breaking it up into pieces with a wooden spoon.
4. Remove the meat from the pan and set aside.
5. Add the onion, garlic and carrot and lower the heat to medium.
6. Sauté the vegetables, scraping the bottom of the pan, until lightly browned.
7. Break the bacon into small pieces and return to the pan along with the ground beef.
8. Add the tomato paste, ketchup, vinegar, soy sauce, sugar, bay leaves and chili flakes and simmer for 15 minutes.
9. Adjust the seasoning with salt and pepper to taste.
10. Pile the mixture onto rolls and serve.

Servings: 6

STACKED HAMBURGER CHILI RICE BOWLS

1 green pepper chopped
1 large onion chopped
1 pound hamburger
2 tablespoons chili powder
2 teaspoons minced garlic
1 tablespoon grape jelly
1 jar tomato sauce
1 can diced tomatoes
1 cup shredded cheddar cheese
3 cups cooked rice
1 cup sour cream
1/2 head lettuce chopped
1 cup salsa
1/2 cup chopped onion
1/2 cup black olives
1 package corn chips

1. To make chili: Brown the hamburger with onion and green pepper. Drain.

2. Add salt and pepper to taste.

3. Add minced garlic and chili powder.

4. Add tomato sauce and diced tomatoes.

5. Add grape jelly and simmer for 30 minutes.

6. To prepare Chili Rice Bowls. Line the bottom of each bowl with corn chips. Add rice and top with chili.

7. Have each individual finish layering their own bowl with sour cream, cheese, chopped onion, salsa and black olives as desired.

Servings: 10

Cooking Times
Preparation Time: 15 minutes
Cooking Time: 30 minutes
Total Time: 45 minutes

SWEET AND SOUR PORK

2 pounds boneless pork loin, cut into 1/2" cubes
1/4 cup soy sauce
Cornmeal
2 or more eggs, beaten
Flour
Oil for frying
1 large onion, cut into eighths
1 large green pepper, cut into 1inch squares
1 cup pineapple chunks, drained (reserve juice)

1. Toss pork cubes with soy sauce. Roll the cubes in cornmeal, then in beaten egg, then in flour. Fry in hot oil until golden brown. Drain on paper towels and keep warm in 350 degree oven.

2. Heat 1 tablespoon oil in wok over high heat. Add onion and stir fry for 2 minutes. Add green pepper and stir fry an additional 2 minutes. Add pineapple and stir fry one minute. Return pork cubes to wok, add sauce and stir until thoroughly heated. Serve with hot, steamed rice.

Servings: 8

Cooking Times
Preparation Time: 15 minutes
Cooking Time: 15 minutes
Total Time: 30 minutes

Continued on next page

Sweet and Sour Pork

Sweet and Sour Sauce

1/2 cup pineapple juice (use juice from canned pineapple chunks)
1/4 cup wine vinegar
2 tablespoons oil
2 tablespoons brown sugar
1 tablespoon soy sauce
1/2 teaspoon pepper
1 teaspoon cornstarch
2 teaspoons water

1. Combine pineapple juice, vinegar, oil, brown sugar, soy sauce and pepper in saucepan. Bring to a boil and add cornstarch which has been mixed with water.

2. Stir until clear and slightly thickened.

Crossing the Three T's of Cooking

Meat

Pasta, Rice & Grains

Coming from a large family and preparing everything in large quantities, I had no idea how to cook for two. When my husband and I were first married, I made a stock pot full of goulash and I think we ate it for one week straight. It took a while, but I can safely say that I can now cook for two, however, most of the time we enjoy leftovers so sometimes I intentionally cook big. One of my granddaughter's favorite recipes is the Cranberry Chicken with Rice. I typically make a huge baking dish so as to purposefully have leftovers for her. A couple of months ago, I made Lasagna for my brother-in-law's family. Even though I snapped this photo before it went in the oven, it still looked so good. The finished product was so tasty that my brother-in-law had a couple of helpings. Of course his wife asked for the recipe and when she prepared it, she made an extra dish to pass onto her neighbors. Everyone liked it, so it was great to see that the recipe worked as well for her.

Lasagna all around...dig in.

BUTTERNUT SQUASH WITH HERBED RICE

1/4 cup butter, softened
Roasted Garlic (See step one)
1 teaspoon fresh oregano
1/2 teaspoon fresh marjoram
1/4 teaspoon ground cinnamon
1/8 teaspoon kosher salt
1/8 teaspoon ground ginger
2 pounds butternut squash peeled and cut into 1-inch cubes
Kosher salt
Freshly ground black pepper
3 tablespoons unsalted butter
2 teaspoons brown sugar, packed
6 cups chicken stock
2 slices maple smoked bacon
1 cup finely chopped shallots or scallions
1 pound uncooked Arborio rice
1 teaspoon snipped fresh sage or 1 teaspoon ground sage
1/2 teaspoon snipped fresh parsley
1/2 teaspoon snipped fresh thyme
1/2 cup white wine
2 tablespoons parsley

Oven Temperature: 325°F

Servings: 10

Cooking Times
Preparation Time: 30 minutes
Cooking Time: 20 minutes

Continued on next page

Butternut Squash with Herbed Rice

1. Place 10 large cloves of unpeeled garlic in a 6-ounce custard cup. Toss cloves with 2 teaspoons extra virgin olive oil and 1 teaspoon water. Season with Kosher salt and ground black pepper. Bake covered in a 325° oven for 35 to 40 minutes, or until garlic is tender. Cool about 15 minutes or until easy to handle. Press garlic out of its skin into another small bowl. With a fork, mash garlic into a puree. Set aside at room temperature until ready to use. Makes 1 to 2 tablespoons.
2. In a small bowl, mix unsalted butter, softened, roasted garlic, oregano, marjoram, ground cinnamon, kosher salt, ground ginger and black pepper.
3. Cover and set aside until ready to serve. Store covered, in the refrigerator in an airtight container. Makes 1/3 cup of herb butter.
4. For caramelized squash, cut squash in half lengthwise. Remove and discard seeds. Peel squash, cut into 3/4 inch cubes. Season squash with kosher salt and black pepper. In a very large skillet, melt butter over medium heat. Add squash.
5. Cook stirring occasionally for 8 to 10 minutes or until browned.
6. Cook covered 5 minutes more or just until tender. Add brown sugar. Cook stirring occasionally about 2 minutes or until squash has caramelized but still holds its shape.
7. Set aside at room temperature until ready to use.
8. In a large saucepan, bring chicken stock to boiling; reduce heat to a very low simmer. In a 4 or 5 quart Dutch oven, cook bacon about 5 minutes or until lightly browned. Add shallots. Cook and stir about 3 minutes or until shallots are tender but not brown. Reduce heat to medium low.
9. Using a wooden spoon, stir rice, sage and thyme into bacon mixture. Cook stirring frequently, 7 to 10 minutes or until the rice is coated and just starts to brown. Add wine. Bring to boiling, reduce heat.
10. Simmer uncovered until wine is absorbed stirring often. Ladle 1 cup of the simmering stock into the rice. Cook stirring frequently, until most of the stock is absorbed.
11. Continue cooking and stirring, adding another 1 cup of stock only when the previous stock is absorbed. After 15 minutes, begin tasting the rice. Add enough remaining stock, about a 1/4 cup at a time until rice is firm yet cooked through, stirring frequently and adding more stock is absorbed.
12. Stir in herb butter and parsley. If you like, season to taste with Kosher salt and black pepper. Gently fold in the caramelized squash. Serve immediately.

Cheese Stuffed Shells

2 eggs, lightly beaten
2 15-ounce container ricotta cheese
2 cups shredded mozzarella cheese (6 ounces)
1 cup grated parmesan cheese
1/2 cup chopped parsley
1/8 teaspoon pepper
1 teaspoon salt
1 12-ounce package jumbo pasta shells
3 cups spaghetti sauce

1. In medium bowl, stir together eggs, ricotta cheese, mozzarella cheese, 3/4 cup parmesan cheese, parsley, salt and pepper.

2. Spoon about 2 tablespoons of the filling into each cooked shell.

3. Arrange in single layer in 13 x 9 x 2 inch baking dish.

4. Spoon spaghetti sauce over shells.

5. Sprinkle with remaining parmesan cheese.

6. Bake in 350° oven for 30 minutes or until heated through.

Oven Temperature: 350°F

Servings: 8
Yield: 64 cups

Cooking Times
Preparation Time: 7 minutes
Cooking Time: 30 minutes
Inactive Time: 5 minutes
Total Time: 42 minutes

Classic Macaroni Salad

4 cups uncooked elbow macaroni
1 cup mayonnaise
1/4 cup distilled white vinegar
2/3 cup white sugar
2 1/2 tablespoons prepared yellow mustard
1 1/2 teaspoon salt
1/2 teaspoon ground black pepper
1 large onion, chopped
2 stalks celery, chopped
1 green bell pepper, seeded and chopped
1/4 cup grated carrot (optional)
2 tablespoons chopped pimento peppers (optional)

1. Bring a large pot of lightly salted water to a boil. Add the macaroni, and cook until tender, about 8 minutes. Rinse under cold water and drain.

2. In a large bowl, mix together the mayonnaise, vinegar, sugar, mustard, salt and pepper.

3. Stir in the onion, celery, green pepper, carrot, pimentos and macaroni.

4. Refrigerate for at least 4 hours before serving, but preferably overnight.

Servings: 10

Cooking Times
Preparation Time: 20 minutes
Cooking Time: 10 minutes
Inactive Time: 4 hours
Total Time: 4 hours and 30 minutes

CRUNCHY CHRISTMAS RICE

2 10-ounce cans chicken broth
1/2 cup water
1 1/2 cups long-grain rice
2 tablespoons butter
1/4 teaspoon salt
1/3 cup chopped celery
1/3 cup chopped onion
1/4 cup chopped parsley
1/4 cup sliced toasted almonds
3 tablespoons drained chopped pimento

1. Combine broth, water, rice and 2 tablespoons butter and salt in large saucepan. Bring to boil; reduce heat.

2. Simmer covered for 18 to 20 minutes or until tender and liquid is absorbed.

3. Sauté celery and onion and 2 tablespoons butter in skillet for 5 minutes or until tender.

4. Stir sautéed vegetables, parsley, almonds, and pimento into hot rice just before serving.

Servings: 8

Cooking Times
Preparation Time: 10 minutes
Cooking Time: 18 minutes
Total Time: 28 minutes

FETTUCCINE ALFREDO

2 teaspoons margarine
3 garlic cloves, chopped
4 1/2 teaspoons flour
1 1/2 cups skim milk
1/2 cup parmesan cheese
3 1/2 teaspoons cream cheese
1/4 teaspoon pepper
4 ounces fettuccine
1/4 cup parsley

1. Melt margarine in medium saucepan.

2. Add garlic, Stir one minute. Stir in flour.

3. Gradually stir in milk.

4. Add cheeses and pepper.

5. Serve over fettuccini topped with parsley.

Servings: 4

Cooking Times
Preparation Time: 10 minutes

GRANOLA

3 cups rolled oats
1/2 cup brown sugar
1/4 cup water
3 tablespoons butter
1 teaspoon vanilla
1/4 cup shredded coconut
1/4 cup wheat germ
1/4 cup sesame seed
1/4 cup slivered almonds

1. Mix all ingredients.
2. Spread on a cookie sheet.
3. Bake at 350° for 20 to 25 minutes.
4. Stir often, cool and store in an airtight container.

Oven Temperature: 350°F

Servings: 8
Yield: 4 cups

Cooking Times
Preparation Time: 10 minutes
Cooking Time: 20 minutes
Total Time: 30 minutes

LASAGNA, SHORT CUT STYLE

1 pound ground beef
1 large tomato diced
1 8-ounce can tomato sauce
2 garlic clove, chopped
1/2 box lasagna noodles
1 6-ounce package mozzarella cheese (add to preference)
1 cup cottage cheese
1/2 cup grated parmesan cheese

1. Brown meat slowly; spoon off excess fat. Add the next 3 ingredients. Cover and simmer 40 minutes, stirring occasionally. Salt and pepper to taste.
2. Cook noodles in boiling salted water till tender. Rinse in cold water and drain.
3. Place noodles in bottom of deep baking dish. Cover bottom with noodles, cover noodles with sauce, and add half the mozzarella cheese.
4. Repeat with a second and third layer.
5. Put remaining sauce on top of last noodles and sprinkle with Parmesan cheeses.
6. Bake in moderate oven 350° for 25 to 30 minutes. Let stand 15 minutes.
7. Cut into squares and serve.

Oven Temperature: 350°F

Servings: 6

Cooking Times
Preparation Time: 40 minutes
Cooking Time: 30 minutes
Inactive Time: 15 minutes
Total Time: 1 hour and 25 minutes

LOBSTER (IMITATION CRAB MEAT) MACARONI AND CHEESE

4 tablespoons butter, plus 1 tablespoon for greasing dish
Kosher salt
1 pound penne pasta
2 small shallots, finely chopped
2 cloves garlic, chopped
Freshly ground black pepper
2 tablespoons tomato paste
5 tablespoons all-purpose flour
1/4 cup white wine
4 cups heavy cream
1/2 teaspoon sweet paprika
1/4 teaspoon cayenne pepper
1 bay leaf
2 cups shredded sharp white Cheddar
2 cups shredded Gruyere
2 8-ounce imitation crab meat
1/4 cup panko bread crumbs
1/4 cup freshly chopped parsley leaves

Oven Temperature: 350°F

Servings: 8

Cooking Times
Preparation Time: 10 minutes
Cooking Time: 1 hour
Inactive Time: 10 minutes

Continued on next page

Lobster (Imitation Crab Meat) Macaroni and Cheese

1. Preheat the oven to 350 degrees F and adjust racks to the middle. Grease a 13 x 9-inch baking dish with butter.

2. In a large pot of boiling salted water over medium heat, add the pasta and cook until al dente. Drain the pasta and reserve.

3. Add 4 tablespoons butter to a large pot over medium heat. Once the butter bubbles, add the shallots and garlic and sauté until translucent. Season with salt and pepper to taste.

4. Add the tomato paste and flour and stir about 3 to 4 minutes. Add the white wine and reduce, by half, about 2 minutes. Slowly whisk in the cream.

5. Add the paprika, cayenne, and bay leaf. Bring the cream up to a simmer and turn the heat to low. Let reduce until the cream is thick. When thickened, remove the bay leaves.

6. Stir in the grated cheeses. Add the crab meat to the sauce and stir well. Add the pasta and stir.

7. Add to the greased baking dish and sprinkle with the panko crumbs and parsley. Bake for 25 minutes. Remove from the oven and let rest for 10 minutes before serving.

8. Sprinkle individual servings with parsley.

Old Fashioned Mac and Cheese

2 cups uncooked elbow macaroni
4 tablespoons butter
2 tablespoons all-purpose flour
2 cups milk
1/4 onion, minced
Salt and pepper to taste
1/4 pound processed cheese food
1/4 pound shredded Cheddar cheese
1/4 pound shredded Swiss cheese

1. Preheat oven to 350 degrees F.

2. Prepare the elbow macaroni according to package directions.

3. Meanwhile, melt the butter in a small saucepan over medium high heat. Stir in the flour until a cream colored paste forms. Then pour in the milk and stir constantly until this comes to a hard boil, and then stir for 1 more minute. Remove from heat and set aside.

4. When the macaroni is cooked, spread 1/2 of it into the bottom of a lightly greased 9x13-inch baking dish. Then layer 1/2 of the minced onion, 1/2 of the salt and pepper and 1/2 of each of the cheeses. Repeat this one more time: macaroni, onion, salt and pepper and cheeses, and then pour the reserved white sauce over all. Top off with small pats of butter to taste.

5. Cover and bake at 350 degrees F for 45 minutes.

Oven Temperature: 350°F

Servings: 7

Cooking Times
Preparation Time: 20 minutes
Cooking Time: 45 minutes

Restaurant Quality Fried Rice

3 green onions, chopped fine

1 cup bean sprouts

1 slice fresh ginger, trimmed, minced, and crushed

3 tablespoons precooked meat, chopped fine*

1 tablespoons peanut oil

3 dashes sesame oil

1 tablespoon soy sauce

1 teaspoon oyster sauce

Dash pepper

2 cups cooked cold white rice

1 egg

Servings: 4

Cooking Times
Preparation Time: 30 minutes
Cooking Time: 15 minutes

Tips:

Cook the rice the night before and chill in refrigerator.

*The meat can be hamburger, ham, shrimp or other seafood, leftover chops or roast (beef, pork, veal, and lamb), any combination of the above, or whatever you might happen to have on hand.

Continued on next page

Restaurant Quality Fried Rice

1. At least three hours before you begin making the fried rice, measure out two cups of rice and cook. Store it in a large, covered bowl overnight in the refrigerator or at least three hours in the freezer.

2. Wash and pick over the bean sprouts. Place in strainer and scald with boiling water. Immediately plunge in ice water. Drain well.

3. While the bean sprouts are draining, chop the green onions fine. Trim, mince, and crush the ginger. Chop the meat.

4. Measure and mix the two kinds of oil.

5. Measure and mix the soy sauce, oyster sauce, and pepper. Beat the egg lightly.

6. Loosen the rice with a fork until all the grains have been separated completely.

7. Preheat the wok on high heat. Add the oil and continue to heat.

8. Add the egg, scrambling and shredding it continuously with a fork.

9. Add the sprouts, onion, meat, and ginger, and stir-fry until most of the liquid is gone.

10. Add the rice, and stir-fry until the rice begins to brown.

11. Add the soy sauce, oyster sauce, and pepper.

12. Stir-fry until everything is thoroughly mixed and the entire contents of the wok are steaming.

Spaghetti Pie

8 ounces spaghetti cooked according to package directions
2 tablespoons cooking oil
2 eggs, beaten
Dash of garlic powder
3/4 cup shredded mozzarella cheese (6 ounces)
1 pound ground beef
1/2 cup chopped onion
1/4 cup chopped green bell pepper
1 15-ounce spaghetti sauce
3/4 teaspoon oregano
3/4 teaspoon fennel seeds
1 cup cottage cheese

1. Cook spaghetti according to package directions; drain.
2. Stir oil, eggs, garlic powder and 1/4 cup of mozzarella cheese into spaghetti.
3. Form spaghetti mixture into a crust in lightly oiled deep dish 10-inch pie plate.
4. In skillet, cook ground beef, onion and green pepper until meat is browned and vegetables are tender.
5. Drain off excess fat and fill spaghetti pie with meat mixture, cover with foil.
6. Bake at 350° for 35 to 40 minutes or until heated through.
7. Uncover, sprinkle with remaining mozzarella cheese.
8. Bake 3 minutes longer or until cheese melts.

Oven Temperature: 350°F

Servings: 6

Cooking Times
Preparation Time: 20 minutes
Cooking Time: 43 minutes
Total Time: 1 hour and 3 minutes

Crossing the Three T's of Cooking

Pasta, Rice & Grains

Pies

I started a tradition of having a pie contest at our family reunion and it was unbelievable the various kinds of pies available for judging as well as the enormous number of pies we all ate. Well, I learned rather quickly that my husband liked any kind of pie and he would often like to sample them all. It became his habit to just simply ask for "one of each". Well that was an impossible request at the family reunion as I would have had to roll him out after he had finished all those

Apple Pie

different kinds of pies. Speaking of apple pie, there is something about it no matter how you make it that it screams family. When my mother made apple pie she used a large roasting pan and filled it to the brim with her homemade filling and topped it off with a rectangle of pie crust. She used to call it her deep dish apple pie. The last time I served apple pie, I had diabetic friends at the table so I made it with a sugar substitute and it was devoured by non-diabetics as well. This year's dessert winner at our family reunion was my ABC pie which I made by doubling the recipe and baking in a rectangle glass baking dish. It was overwhelmingly devoured with only a few traces of berries left on the bottom of the pan.

ABC Pie (Apple, Blueberry, and Cherry)

1 pastry for double crust 9-inch pie
1 12-ounce package blueberries, frozen or 2 cups fresh
1 12-ounce package cherries, frozen or 2 cups fresh
2 cups chopped apples
1 cup sugar
4 teaspoons quick cooking tapioca
2 tablespoons cornstarch
1/2 teaspoon ground cinnamon
1/2 teaspoon ground nutmeg
1 lemon zested and juiced
4 tablespoons butter

1. Prepare pastry.
2. In large mixing bowl, stir together the sugar, tapioca, cornstarch, cinnamon, and nutmeg and lemon zest.
3. Add the blueberries, cherries, and apples and lemon juice. Toss gently until coated.
4. Let stand 15 minutes.
5. Spoon filling into pastry-lined pie plate. Dot with butter. Trim pastry even with the edge of the pie plate. Trim top crust to 1/2 inch beyond edge of pie plate. Fold top pastry and crimp edge. Cover edge of pie with foil to prevent over browning.
6. Bake in 375° oven for 25 minutes. Remove foil. Bake for 20 to 25 minutes more or until the crust is golden brown and the filling is bubbling. Cool on a wire rack.

Oven Temperature: 375°F

Servings: 8

Cooking Times
Preparation Time: 25 minutes
Cooking Time: 50 minutes
Inactive Time: 1 hour
Total Time: 2 hours and 15 minutes

ANN'S RAISIN SQUARE

    2 pounds raisins
    1 cup sugar
    1/2 teaspoon cinnamon
    1/2 teaspoon nutmeg
    3 large Granny Smith apples diced
    2 tablespoons of flour or cornstarch added to water

1. Mix all ingredients together in a large saucepan.
2. Cover with water and heat to boiling.
3. Thicken mixture with flour and water or cornstarch and water until thick.
4. Let cool.
5. Make pie crust for large cookie sheet.
6. Line the bottom and sides of pan.
7. Pour mixture on crust and make top crust, just like a pie.
8. Sprinkle sugar on top and bake at 375° for 45 minutes.
9. Frost with white cream cheese frosting if desired. Cut into squares and serve.

Servings: 24
Yield: 24 pieces

Cooking Times
Preparation Time: 20 minutes
Cooking Time: 45 minutes
Total Time: 1 hour and 5 minutes

Deep Dish Apple Pie

Filling

10 cups apples, cored and sliced into 8 wedges each	1/2 teaspoon cinnamon
1 cup sugar	1/2 teaspoon salt
1 tablespoon flour	1/2 teaspoon nutmeg
	3 tablespoons butter

1. Peel and slice apples for pie.
2. Mix sugar, flour, cinnamon, salt and nutmeg together and sprinkle over the apples that have been placed in pie plate.
3. Dot with the butter.

Dough

1 cup flour	1/3 cup shortening
1/2 teaspoon salt	3 tablespoons cold milk

1. Make dough by mixing flour, salt, and shortening. Blend.
2. Add cold milk. Roll out dough, handle as little as possible.
3. Place over apples and flute edges.
4. Brush on milk for golden crust. Sprinkle with sugar.
5. Slash pie dough for air vents.
6. Bake 50 minutes at 400°.

Oven Temperature: 400°F

Servings: 8

Cooking Times
Cooking Time: 50 minutes

Esther's Perfect Apple Pie

    1 box refrigerated pie crust
    6 cups apples, peeled, sliced
    3/4 cup sugar
    2 tablespoons flour
    3/4 teaspoon cinnamon
    1/4 teaspoon salt
    1/8 teaspoon freshly grated nutmeg
    1 tablespoon lemon juice
    Butter

1. Heat oven to 425°.
2. Place one pie crust in 9-inch pie plate.
3. In large bowl, gently mix filling ingredients, spoon into pie plate.
4. Dot with butter and sprinkle with lemon juice.
5. Place on top crust, cut slits for air to escape.
6. Bake 40 to 45 minutes or until apples are tender.
7. You may cover edges with aluminum foil to prevent too much browning.

Servings: 8
Yield: 1 pie

Cooking Times
Preparation Time: 20 minutes
Cooking Time: 40 minutes
Total Time: 1 hour

FRESH BLUEBERRY PIE

5 cups blueberries
1 tablespoon lemon juice
1 pastry for double crust 9-inch pie
1 cup sugar
1/3 cup all purpose flour
1/8 teaspoon salt
1/2 teaspoon ground cinnamon
2 tablespoons butter
1 large egg, lightly beaten
1 teaspoon sugar

1. Sprinkle berries with lemon juice, set aside.

2. Roll half of pastry to 1/8 inch thickness on a floured surface. Place in a 9-inch pie plate.

3. Combine 1 cup sugar and next 3 ingredients; add to berries, stirring well. Pour into pastry shell, and dot with butter.

4. Roll remaining pastry to 1/8 inch thickness. Place over filling, seal and crimp edges.

5. Cut slits in top of crust to allow steam to escape. Brush top of pastry with beaten egg, and sprinkle with 1 teaspoon sugar.

6. Bake at 400° for 35 minutes or until golden. Cover edges with aluminum foil to prevent over browning.

Oven Temperature: 400°F

Servings: 8

Cooking Times
Preparation Time: 15 minutes
Cooking Time: 35 minutes
Inactive Time: 2 hours
Total Time: 2 hours and 50 minutes

Tips:
You can use the rolled pie crusts in the refrigerated section of the grocery store or the pie shells in the frozen section. They work great.

Fresh Peach Pie

5 1/2 cups peaches, pitted and thinly sliced
1 cup sugar
1/4 cup all purpose flour
1/2 teaspoon ground cinnamon
3 tablespoons butter
1 teaspoon vanilla extract
1 pastry for double crust 9-inch pie

1. Mix all ingredients in a bowl. Gently toss to coat peaches.

2. Spoon filling into prepared pie crust. Brush bottom crust with water around the edge and place top crust on.

3. Crimp edges and cut slits for air vents in top crust.

4. Bake at 425° for 15 minutes. Reduce heat to 350° and bake for 25 to 30 minutes or until crust is browned and filling bubbly.

Servings: 8

Cooking Times
Preparation Time: 38 minutes
Cooking Time: 55 minutes
Inactive Time: 1 hour
Total Time: 2 hours and 33 minutes

FRESH RHUBARB PIE

Pastry for double crust 9-inch pie
1 1/3 cups sugar
5 cups sliced rhubarb, (1 inch pieces) fresh
1/4 cup cornstarch
2 tablespoons butter
2 teaspoons sugar

1. Roll half of pastry to 1/8 inch thickness on a lightly floured surface.

2. Place in a 9-inch pie plate; trim off excess pastry along edges.

3. Cover with plastic wrap, and chill until ready to fill.

4. Combine 1 1/3 cups sugar, cornstarch, and nutmeg, stirring until blended; stir in rhubarb, and let stand 15 minutes. Spoon mixture into pastry shell, dot with butter.

5. Roll remaining pastry to 1/8 inch thickness; cut into 1/2 inch strips. Arrange strips in lattice design over filling. Trim strips even with edges; fold edges under, and crimp. Sprinkle top of pastry with 2 teaspoons sugar.

6. Bake at 425° for 15 minutes; reduce heat to 350° and bake 30 more minutes or until crust is browned.

Servings: 8

Cooking Times
Preparation Time: 25 minutes
Cooking Time: 45 minutes
Total Time: 1 hour and 10 minutes

Tips:

For Strawberry-Rhubarb Pie: Follow recipe above, substituting 2 1/2 cups thickly sliced strawberries for half of rhubarb and reducing sugar to 1 cup.

Fresh Strawberry Pie

1/4 cup cornstarch
1 1/2 cup water
1 1/2 cup sugar
1 3-ounce box strawberry gelatin
2 cups strawberries, washed and stemmed
1 cooked pie shell
Whipped cream

1. Cook cornstarch, water, and sugar until clear.

2. Add small box of gelatin.

3. Cool.

4. Pour over whole berries in a cooked pie shell. Cut into slices and top with whipped cream

Servings: 8
Yield: 1 pie

Cooking Times
Preparation Time: 15 minutes
Cooking Time: 5 minutes
Inactive Time: 30 minutes
Total Time: 50 minutes

Pumpkin Pie

1 unbaked 9-inch deep-dish pie shell
2 cups canned pumpkin
1 15-ounce can sweetened condensed milk
1 egg
1/2 teaspoon salt
1/2 teaspoon nutmeg
1/2 teaspoon ginger
3/4 teaspoon cinnamon

1. In large size mixing bowl, blend together all ingredients.

2. Turn mixture into pie shell.

3. Bake at 375° until sharp-bladed knife comes out clean.

4. Cool, refrigerate at least 1 hour.

Oven Temperature: 375°F

Servings: 8
Yield: 1 9 inch pie

Cooking Times
Preparation Time: 10 minutes
Cooking Time: 50 minutes
Total Time: 1 hour

Sweet Potato Pie

1 pound sweet potato, peeled and cubed
1 1/4 cups plain yogurt
3/4 cup dark brown sugar, packed
1 9-inch deep dish frozen pie shell
1 tablespoon maple syrup
1 cup chopped pecans
1/2 teaspoon cinnamon
1/4 teaspoon nutmeg
5 egg yolks
Salt

1. Put cubed potatoes into steam basket and place steamer basket into a large pot of simmering water that is no closer than 2 inches from the bottom of the basket.
2. Allow to steam for 20 minutes or until the potatoes are fork tender.
3. Mash with potato masher and set aside.
4. Preheat oven to 350 degrees.
5. Place sweet potatoes in the bowl of a stand mixer and heat with the paddle attachment.
6. Add yogurt, brown sugar, cinnamon, nutmeg, yolks, and salt to taste.
7. Beat until well combined.
8. Pour this batter into the pie shell and place onto a sheet pan.
9. Sprinkle pecans on top and drizzle with maple syrup.
10. Bake for 50 to 55 minutes.
11. Remove from oven and cool. Keep refrigerated after cooling.

Oven Temperature: 350°F

Servings: 8

Crossing the Three T's of Cooking

Pies

Poultry

At Christmas time, my husband's family takes turns hosting the family gathering. When I had only been married a year, I decided I would take my turn. Traditionally, the hostess made turkey and ham but since I had never cooked a turkey on my own, I announced that I was doing something different. My husband's aunt showed signs of dismay that the idea might not be acceptable. So she politely handed me the cash to buy a turkey and said I could cook it myself...it's not that hard. Well, I think every cook has done this at least once in her lifetime...yes, I am talking about roasting the bird with the bagged giblets inside and I was no exception. My cooking skills have since progressed to being able to prepare turkey in any fashion, but my favorite now is my husband's smoked turkey on the grill. It is marinated and develops a smoky flavor that is beyond belief and the leftovers make great smoked turkey noodle soup.

Smoked Turkey

BAKED CHICKEN BREASTS SUPREME

1 1/2 cups plain yogurt or sour cream
1/4 cup lemon juice
1/2 teaspoon Worcestershire sauce
1/2 teaspoon celery seed
1/8 teaspoon paprika
1 clove garlic, minced
1/2 teaspoon salt
1/4 teaspoon pepper
8 boneless skinless chicken breast halves
2 cups fine dry bread crumbs

1. In a large bowl, combine first eight ingredients.
2. Place chicken in mixture and turn to coat.
3. Cover and marinate overnight in the refrigerator.
4. Remove chicken from marinade, coat each piece with crumbs.
5. Arrange on shallow baking pan.
6. Bake uncovered at 350° for 45 minutes or until juices run clear.

Oven Temperature: 350°F

Servings: 8

Cooking Times
Preparation Time: 20 minutes
Cooking Time: 45 minutes
Inactive Time: 9 hours
Total Time: 10 hours and 5 minutes

BRINE FOR TURKEY

1 1/4 cup salt
1 quart hot water
4 cups cold water
1 cup maple syrup
1 medium onion thinly sliced

4 cloves garlic, crushed
10 peppercorns
5 bay leaves
4 strips lemon zest
2 cloves

1. Place salt and 1 quart of hot water in large deep pot and whisk until salt crystals are dissolved.
2. Whisk in cold water and maple syrup and add the onion, garlic, peppercorns, bay leaves, lemon zest, and cloves. The mixture should be no warmer than room temperature.
3. Add the turkey.
4. Place in large zip lock bag to keep the turkey submerged. Place in refrigerator and let marinate overnight.
5. Set up grill for indirect grilling and preheat to medium. Place turkey on the grate over a drip pan.
6. Brush with melted butter. Indirect grill until cooked, 2 1/2 to 3 hours. Use an instant read thermometer to test for doneness (180°).
7. Baste the turkey with melted butter every hour.
8. Transfer turkey to a cutting board and let rest for 10 to 15 minutes before carving.

Oven Temperature: 275°F

Yield: Enough brine for 12 pound turkey

Cooking Times
Preparation Time: 15 minutes
Cooking Time: 2 hours
Inactive Time: 20 hours
Total Time: 22 hours and 15 minutes

CHICKEN AND BISCUITS CASSEROLE

1/2 cup onion chopped
1/3 cup butter
1/3 cup flour
3 cups chicken broth
4 cups chopped cooked chicken
1 1/2 teaspoon salt
1 cup cooked peas
1/2 cup mushrooms sliced
1/4 cup pimientos chopped
1 can refrigerated biscuits

1. Brown onion in butter.
2. Add the rest of ingredients.
3. Top with cut up biscuits.
4. Bake at 350° for about 35 minutes or until bubbly.

Servings: 8

Cooking Times
Cooking Time: 35 minutes
Inactive Time: 10 minutes
Total Time: 45 minutes

Chicken Pot Pie

2 frozen pie shells
2 large potatoes peeled and cut into 1/2-inch cubes
2 large carrots peeled and thinly sliced
2/3 cup green peas
2 cans cream of chicken soup
2 cups chicken breasts
2 tablespoons onion chopped
1 teaspoon salt
Black pepper
1 teaspoon sage

1. Line a pie plate with one of the pie crusts.
2. In a large bowl mix all ingredients well.
3. Pour into the prepared crust and place on the top crust.
4. Preheat oven to 375 degrees.
5. Poke holes in the top of the pie crust.
6. Brush melted butter over the top of the pie.
7. Bake for 30 to 35 minutes until golden brown.

Servings: 6

Cooking Times

Preparation Time: 20 minutes
Cooking Time: 30 minutes
Total Time: 50 minutes

CRANBERRY CHICKEN

1 11-ounce can jellied cranberry sauce
1 12-ounce bottle Catalina Dressing
1 envelope onion soup mix
8 3-ounce chicken breasts

1. Lay chicken breasts in 13 x 9 inch pan.

2. Mix cranberry sauce, Catalina dressing, onion soup mix together in blender.

3. Pour over chicken.

4. Cover with foil.

5. Bake for approximately 40 to 60 minutes depending on the thickness of chicken.

6. Serve over rice.

Servings: 8

Cooking Times
Preparation Time: 10 minutes
Total Time: 1 hour and 10 minutes

Golden Glazed Turkey with Sausage and Mushroom Stuffing and Perfect Turkey Gravy

1 10-pound Turkey
1/2 cup melted butter
1/4 cup honey
1 tablespoon soy sauce

1. Preheat oven to 325°. Stuff turkey with mushroom and sausage stuffing. Truss turkey.

2. Place turkey breast side up on rack in shallow roasting pan. Brush with melted butter.

3. Roast, loosely covered with foil, for 4 1/2 hours. Baste turkey with mixture of 2 tablespoons butter, honey and soy sauce.

4. Roast for 15 minutes longer or to 180° on meat thermometer.

5. Let stand, covered with foil.

6. Arrange slices on serving platter, serve with Perfect turkey gravy.

Servings: 10

Cooking Times
Preparation Time: 10 minutes
Cooking Time: 4 hours and 30 minutes
Inactive Time: 20 minutes
Total Time: 5 hours

Continued on next page

Golden Glazed Turkey with Sausage and Mushroom Stuffing and Perfect Turkey Gravy

Perfect Turkey Gravy

4 1/2 cups turkey stock
1/2 cup flour
1 teaspoon Kitchen Bouquet
1 teaspoon salt
1/8 teaspoon freshly ground black pepper
2 tablespoons turkey drippings or chicken broth

1. Blend 1 cup cold stock with flour in small bowl.

2. Heat remaining 3 1/2 cups stock in saucepan. Stir in flour mixture.

3. Cook until thickened, stirring constantly. Reduce heat to low.

4. Add seasonings, drippings. Cook for 2 to 3 minutes longer. Yield 4 cups.

Mushroom and Sausage Stuffing

1 1/2 cup chopped celery	8 ounces pork sausage
1 cup chopped mushrooms	1/2 cup melted butter
10 cups torn day old bread	1 cup chopped onion
2 tablespoons chopped parsley	1 teaspoon salt
2 teaspoons poultry seasoning	1/4 teaspoon pepper
1 teaspoon chicken flavored stock base	1 cup boiling water

1. Brown sausage with celery, onion, mushrooms parsley, salt, and seasoning in butter.

2. Add chicken stock base and boiling water.

3. Pour over bread mixture, toss lightly.

4. Fill turkey or bake separately at 325° for 1 hour. Makes 10 to 12 servings.

Mayonnaise Crusted Chicken

1/2 cup really good mayonnaise
1/4 cup parmesan cheese, grated
4 boneless chicken breast halves
4 teaspoons bread crumbs

1. Combine mayonnaise and parmesan cheese.
2. Spread on chicken.
3. Sprinkle on bread crumbs.
4. Bake at 425° for 20 minutes.
5. Cover loosely with aluminum foil.
6. Bake 20 to 25 minutes longer.

Oven Temperature: 425°F

Servings: 4

Cooking Times
Preparation Time: 10 minutes
Cooking Time: 45 minutes
Total Time: 55 minutes

Tips:
I like to use the frozen chicken tenders.

Restaurant Quality Orange Chicken

1 1/2 cups water
2 tablespoons orange juice
1/4 cup lemon juice
1/3 cup rice vinegar
2 1/2 tablespoons soy sauce
1 tablespoon grated orange zest
1 cup packed brown sugar
1/2 teaspoon minced fresh ginger root
1/2 teaspoon minced garlic
2 tablespoons chopped green onion
1/4 teaspoon red pepper flakes
3 tablespoons cornstarch
2 tablespoons water
2 boneless, skinless chicken breasts cut into 1/2 inch pieces
1 cup all-purpose flour
1/4 teaspoon salt
1/4 teaspoon pepper
3 tablespoons olive oil

Servings: 4

Cooking Times
Preparation Time: 40 minutes
Cooking Time: 40 minutes

Continued on next page

Restaurant Quality Orange Chicken

1. Pour 1 1/2 cups water, orange juice, lemon juice, rice vinegar, and soy sauce into a saucepan and set over medium-high heat. Stir in the orange zest, brown sugar, ginger, garlic, chopped onion, and red pepper flakes. Mix cornstarch and water and add to sauce. Bring to a boil. Remove from heat, and cool 10 to 15 minutes.

2. Place the chicken pieces into a re-sealable plastic bag. When contents of saucepan have cooled, pour 1 cup of sauce into bag. Reserve the remaining sauce. Seal the bag, and refrigerate at least 2 hours.

3. In another re-sealable plastic bag, mix the flour, salt, and pepper. Add the marinated chicken pieces, seal the bag, and shake to coat.

4. Heat the olive oil in a large skillet over medium heat. Place chicken into the skillet, and brown on both sides. Drain on a plate lined with paper towels, and cover with aluminum foil.

5. In a clean skillet, add the sauce. Bring to a boil over medium-high heat. Mix together the cornstarch and 2 tablespoons water; stir into the sauce. Reduce heat to medium low; add the chicken pieces, and simmer, about 5 minutes, stirring occasionally.

6. Serve with fried rice.

Sausage and Pecan Dressing Casserole

    8 ounces pork sausage
    1 cup finely chopped celery
    1/2 cup chopped onion
    1/2 cup butter
    2 6-ounce packages of crouton stuffing mix
    3 cups broth or water
    1/2 cup chopped pecans

1. Crumble sausage into 3-quart glass casserole.
2. Microwave covered on high for 2 minutes or until brown; drain.
3. Microwave celery, onion, and butter in covered casserole for 4 minutes until tender.
4. Combine stuffing mix, celery mixture and broth in a large bowl, mix lightly. Stir in sausage and chopped pecans.
5. Microwave on high for 10 minutes.

Servings: 12

SMOKED TURKEY

Juice to Inject Into Turkey

1 pint apple juice

2 tablespoons pickling salt

2 tablespoons honey

3/4 teaspoon meat tenderizer

1/2 teaspoon white pepper

1. Heat the apple juice, salt, pepper and meat tenderizer to 160 degrees. Allow the brine to cool a bit, add the honey, stirring until dissolved.

2. Inject about one ounce of the brine per pound of turkey weight into the leg, thigh, and breast.

3. Insert the needle fully, and then begin to slowly inject the brine as the needle is being pulled out.

4. Add brine to different areas by pulling the needle out partially, then pushing it back in to a different spot.

5. Smoke at 325 degrees for 10 minutes per pound using apple wood for smoke.

6. Wrap with foil and continue smoking until the thigh reaches 175 degrees.

7. Remove the turkey from the grill and let it rest for an hour before serving.

Oven Temperature: 325°F

Servings: 16
Yield: 12 pound Turkey

Cooking Times
Preparation Time: 20 minutes
Cooking Time: 2 hours
Inactive Time: 48 hours
Total Time: 50 hours and 20 minutes

Sweet Potato Stuffing with Bacon and Thyme

10 cups 1-inch sour dough bread cubes
1 pound thick cut bacon
2 tablespoons butter
6 1/2 cups peeled and cubed sweet potatoes
2 large onions cubed
3 cups celery in 1/2 to 3/4 inch pieces
1 1/2 tablespoons fresh thyme leaves
1 1/2 cups orange juice
1 1/4 teaspoons kosher salt
3 large eggs
1 1/2 cups chicken broth

1. Bake bread cubes for 10 minutes at 350°.
2. Place bread in a large bowl.
3. Cook bacon, save 3 tablespoon of drippings.
4. Add butter, sweet potatoes, onions, celery, thyme, salt and sauté until slightly soft but not brown.
5. Add orange juice, cook until potatoes are tender.
6. Add bacon and sweet potato mixture to bread.
7. Season with salt and black pepper.
8. Add eggs to chicken broth and whisk. Add to stuffing mixture.
9. Bake at 350° for 50 minutes to 1 hour.

Oven Temperature: 350°F

Servings: 8

Cooking Times
Preparation Time: 20 minutes
Cooking Time: 50 minutes
Total Time: 1 hour and 10 minutes

Turkey Apple Sausage

1 beaten egg white
1/4 bread crumbs
1/4 cup apple chopped
1/4 teaspoon salt
1/4 teaspoon ground sage
1/8 teaspoon ground pepper
1/2 pound ground turkey

1. In a medium mixing bowl combine egg white, bread crumbs, apple, salt, sage, and pepper.

2. Add ground turkey; mix well.

3. Shape into eight small patties, about 2 1/2 inches in diameter.

4. Place sausage patties on the unheated rack of a broiler pan. Broil 4 to 5 inches from the heat for 4 minutes. Turn and broil for 4 to 5 minutes more or until no longer pink.

5. Pat sausage patties with paper towels. Arrange on serving plate. Garnish with apple slices if desired.

Servings: 4

Cooking Times
Preparation Time: 10 minutes
Cooking Time: 10 minutes

Tips:
These may also be pan fried in olive oil.

Crossing the Three T's of Cooking

Poultry

Salads & Dressings

My guests have enjoyed several kinds of green salads with my homemade salad dressings and invariably I will get asked for the recipe. There is nothing like fresh spinach mixed with Romaine lettuce. At Christmas time I switch to a shredded lettuce for my Christmas salad. It is simply placing the shredded lettuce on a platter that has been topped with chopped tomatoes, green and red peppers, cucumbers, and other choices displayed in a swirl pattern. That way each guest selects what vegetables they desire. I have included my recipe for potato salad to which I have added all kinds of chopped vegetables successfully, but our favorite is just potatoes, eggs and my dressing. The Classic Macaroni Salad is a favorite and my husband enjoys it even more when I add the chopped crab. Recently when I made it, he reminded me to keep the fixings for that salad in the house at all times.

Orange Cauliflower Salad

ABSOLUTELY WONDERFUL GREEK DRESSING

    1 1/2 quarts olive oil
    1/3 cup garlic powder
    1/3 cup dried oregano
    1/3 cup dried basil
    1/4 cup pepper
    1/4 cup salt
    1/4 cup onion powder
    1/4 cup Dijon-style mustard
    2 quarts red wine vinegar

1. In a very large container, mix together the olive oil, garlic powder, oregano, basil, pepper, salt, onion powder, and Dijon-style mustard.

2. Pour in the vinegar, and mix vigorously until well blended. Store tightly covered at room temperature.

Servings: 16

Cooking Times
Preparation Time: 10 minutes
Total Time: 10 minutes

AMBROSIA SALAD

2 6-ounce cans mandarin oranges
1 15-ounce can pineapple tidbits
1 cup coconut
1 cup marshmallows
1 cup sour cream
1 package dry whipped topping

1. Drain mandarin oranges and pineapple.

2. Mix sour cream with the dry whipped topping mix.

3. Add coconut and marshmallows. Stir.

4. Put in bowl to serve.

Servings: 10
Yield: 40 ounces

Cooking Times
Preparation Time: 20 minutes
Total Time: 20 minutes

Tips:
You may use colored marshmallows for the springtime.

BLACK BEAN SALAD

1/2 cup Ranch Dressing
1 cup black beans
1 11-ounce can whole kernel corn
1 cup grape or cherry tomatoes
1/2 cup chopped red onion
2 tablespoons fresh cilantro chopped
Hot pepper sauce, to taste

1. In medium bowl, combine all ingredients, chill.
2. Garnish if desired, with lime wedges.

Servings: 4

Cooking Times
Preparation Time: 10 minutes
Inactive Time: 30 minutes

BLENDER MAYONNAISE

1 egg
2 tablespoons vinegar
3/4 teaspoon salt
1/2 teaspoon dry mustard
1/4 teaspoon paprika
1/2 teaspoon salad herbs (optional)
1 cup salad oil

1. Have all ingredients room temperature. Put egg, 1 tablespoon vinegar, salt, dry mustard, paprika and salad herbs (if desired) in blender container; cover and blend on Speed 2.

2. While blender is running on Speed 2, slowly pour in 1/2 cup salad oil through opening in cover.

3. When more power is required, run on Speed 7. Stop blender and push ingredients toward blades with rubber spatula if necessary.

4. Add remaining 1 tablespoon vinegar and slowly pour in remaining salad oil while blender is running on Speed 7.

Servings: 6
Yield: 1 cup

Cooking Times
Preparation Time: 10 minutes
Total Time: 10 minutes

Carrot Salad

2 cups shredded carrot
1 cup shredded cabbage
1/2 cup raisins plumped
1 tablespoon lemon juice
1/2 teaspoon salt
1/2 cup mayonnaise

1. Plump raisins by covering with hot water and letting stand for 5 minutes. Drain well.//
2. Combine shredded carrot and cabbage, raisins, lemon juice and salt.
3. Mix well and add mayonnaise.
4. Toss to mix well. Chill until ready to serve.

Servings: 6

Cooking Times
Preparation Time: 10 minutes
Inactive Time: 5 minutes
Total Time: 15 minutes

COLESLAW DRESSING

1/2 cup mayonnaise
3/4 teaspoon salt
Speck pepper
Dash paprika
1/2 teaspoon sugar
1 tablespoon vinegar
1 tablespoon milk

1. Blend all ingredients; refrigerate.
2. Use for 2 cups cabbage slaw.

Servings: 4
Yield: 1/2 cup

Cooking Times
Preparation Time: 5 minutes

Fluffy Fruit Salad

2 20-ounce cans crushed pineapple
2 tablespoons all purpose flour
1 tablespoon vegetable oil
2 16-ounce cans fruit cocktail
2 11-ounce cans mandarin oranges
1 cup heavy whipping cream

2/3 cup sugar
2 eggs
1/4 cup orange juice
3 tablespoons lemon juice
2 bananas, sliced

1. Drain pineapple, reserving 1 cup juice.

2. In a small pan add juice, sugar, flour, eggs, orange juice, lemon juice and oil.

3. Bring to a boil, stirring constantly. Boil for 1 minute. Remove from heat and let cool.

4. In a salad bowl, combine pineapple, fruit cocktail, oranges, and bananas. Fold in whipped cream and cooled sauce.

5. Chill for several hours.

Servings: 12

Cooking Times
Preparation Time: 20 minutes
Cooking Time: 1 minute
Inactive Time: 2 hours
Total Time: 2 hours and 21 minutes

FRENCH DRESSING

1 large onion, coarsely chopped
1/2 cup catsup
1 cup oil
1/2 cup vinegar
3/4 cup sugar
1/2 teaspoon garlic salt

1. Coarsely chop onion.

2. Blend all ingredients in blender.

3. Chill.

Servings: 24
Yield: 3 cups

Cooking Times
Preparation Time: 15 minutes
Total Time: 15 minutes

FRESH BROCCOLI SALAD

Salad

1 large broccoli florets cut into small pieces
1/2 small red onion
4 slices bacon
1/2 cup raisins
3/4 cup sunflower seeds

1. Combine all ingredients in serving bowl.

Dressing

1 cup salad dressing
2 tablespoons vinegar
1 teaspoon sugar
1/2 teaspoon lemon seasoning
Fresh or dried chives

1. Combine dressing ingredients and stir into salad.
2. Refrigerate for 2 hours before serving.

Servings: 10

Grandma Conlin's Slumgullion Fruit Salad

1 cup Grape Nuts cereal
1 15-ounce can crushed pineapple
1 cup grapes sliced in half
1 cup apples, peeled, cored and diced
1 6-ounce can mandarin oranges (drained)
1 4-ounce jar maraschino cherries sliced in half
2 bananas, sliced
1 8-ounce frozen whipped topping
Pecans or walnuts, halved, if desired

1. Drain pineapple and mix juice with Grape Nuts cereal and let sit overnight in the refrigerator. (Cereal will absorb liquid).

2. Just before serving mix in grapes, pineapple, nuts, mandarin oranges, bananas, cherries, and apples.

3. Mix well with frozen whipped topping and serve immediately.

Servings: 16

Cooking Times
Preparation Time: 20 minutes
Total Time: 20 minutes

Tips:
Use fresh fruit and a good quality whipped topping.

Homemade Buttermilk Ranch Dressing

1 cup buttermilk
1/2 cup mayonnaise
1 teaspoon lemon juice
1/8 teaspoon paprika
1/4 teaspoon mustard powder
1/2 teaspoon salt
1/8 teaspoon black pepper
1 tablespoon chopped fresh parsley
1 teaspoon chopped fresh chives
1/4 teaspoon of dry dill (or a teaspoon chopped fresh)

1. In a medium bowl, stir together the buttermilk and mayonnaise until fully mixed.
2. Add in the other ingredients, adjusting for taste.

Servings: 12
Yield: 1 1/2 cups

Cooking Times
Preparation Time: 10 minutes
Total Time: 10 minutes

Hot Chicken Salad

2 cups cooked chicken breast meat, cubed
1 cup diced celery
1/2 cup slivered almonds or water chestnuts
1/2 teaspoon salt
1/2 teaspoon pepper
2 tablespoons fresh lemon juice
1 cup mayonnaise
1 cup grated sharp cheddar cheese
2/3 cup crushed potato chips

1. Preheat oven to 350 degrees F. Spray a 13 by 9-inch baking dish with vegetable oil cooking spray.

2. In a large mixing bowl combine the chicken, celery, almonds, salt, pepper, lemon juice, mayonnaise, and cheese. Place the mixture in the prepared baking dish.

3. Spread the crushed potato chips on top.

4. Bake for 20 minutes, or until bubbly.

Oven Temperature: 350°F

Servings: 8

Cooking Times
Preparation Time: 10 minutes
Cooking Time: 20 minutes
Total Time: 30 minutes

Margie's Sauerkraut Salad

1 quart sauerkraut, drained
1 onion, chopped
2 stalks celery, chopped
1 green bell pepper, chopped
1 large carrot, chopped
1 4-ounce jar diced pimento peppers, drained
1 teaspoon mustard seed
1 1/2 cups white sugar
1 cup vegetable oil
1/2 cup cider vinegar

1. In a large bowl, mix together sauerkraut, onion, celery, green bell pepper, carrot, pimentos, and mustard seed. Set aside this mixture.

2. In a small saucepan, mix together sugar, oil, and vinegar. Bring to a boil. Remove from heat.

3. Pour sugar mixture over salad, cover, and leave it in the refrigerator for 2 days before serving.

Servings: 6

Cooking Times
Preparation Time: 10 minutes

Mary's Potato Salad

8 potatoes, peeled and cubed
8 eggs boiled, peeled, cubed
1 1/2 cup really good mayonnaise
1 tablespoon yellow mustard
1 tablespoon honey
1 teaspoon dill weed
1 teaspoon paprika
1 teaspoon celery seeds
Salt and pepper to taste

1. Cook potatoes with skins on, let cool, peel and cube.
2. Bring eggs to a boil; turn off heat, let sit for 18 minutes.
3. Peel eggs and cube.
4. Place eggs and potatoes in a mixing bowl and season with salt and pepper.
5. Mix mayonnaise, mustard, honey and seasonings together with a wire whisk.
6. Pour on potatoes and eggs and mix well.
7. Chill before serving.

Servings: 8
Yield: 10 cups

Tips:
You may add onion, celery and radishes if desired.

ORANGE CAULIFLOWER SALAD

    2 11-ounce cans mandarin oranges
    2 cups cauliflower florets
    2 cups spinach uncooked
    1/4 cup green pepper chopped
    1/4 cup French salad dressing

1. Toss orange segments, cauliflower florets, green pepper, spinach, and salad dressing.
2. Serve in lettuce cups or in a large bowl.

Servings: 6
Yield: 6

Cooking Times
Preparation Time: 20 minutes
Total Time: 20 minutes

ORIENTAL SALAD

1 16-ounce package broccoli slaw mix
2 bunches green onion chopped
1 cup sunflower seeds
1 cup slivered almonds
2 packages Beef flavored Ramen noodles
1/3 cup oil
1/2 cup sugar
1/3 cup vinegar

1. Mix broccoli, green onions, almonds, sunflower seeds and broken up ramen noodles.
2. Mix oil, sugar, and vinegar and stir into salad.

Servings: 8
Yield: 8 cups

Cooking Times
Preparation Time: 10 minutes
Total Time: 10 minutes

RUSSIAN SALAD DRESSING

1/2 cup mayonnaise
3 tablespoons ketchup
2 tablespoons sweet pickle relish
1 tablespoon horseradish

1. In a small bowl, combine all ingredients. Stir until well blended.

2. Refrigerate in an airtight container.

Servings: 4
Yield: 3/4 cup

Cooking Times
Preparation Time: 10 minutes
Total Time: 10 minutes

Seven-Layer Salad

1 head lettuce, shredded
6 eggs boiled
10 slices crumbled bacon
1 1/2 cup shredded cheese
1 package frozen peas
1 8-ounce container sour cream
1 cup really good mayonnaise

1. Shred lettuce, cheese.

2. Chop boiled eggs, crumble bacon.

3. Layer items and top with 1 cup of mayonnaise and sour cream mixed.

Servings: 10

Cooking Times
Preparation Time: 15 minutes

Spinach and Strawberry Salad

　　1 pound fresh spinach leaves, trimmed and torn
　　1 pint strawberries, sliced
　　1/2 cup sugar
　　1 tablespoon poppy seeds
　　1 1/2 teaspoon paprika
　　1/4 cup wine vinegar
　　1/4 teaspoon Worcestershire sauce
　　1/2 cup salad oil

1. Blend sugar, poppy seed, paprika, wine vinegar, and Worcestershire sauce.

2. Add salad oil to mixture.

3. Pour over chilled spinach.

4. Slice strawberries and add to salad.

Servings: 8

Cooking Times
Preparation Time: 15 minutes
Total Time: 15 minutes

Strawberry Apple Salsa Salad

- 1 pint strawberries, sliced
- 1 medium McIntosh apple, chopped
- 1 medium Granny Smith apple, chopped
- 2 tablespoons sliced green onions
- 2 tablespoons chopped cilantro
- 3/4 cup raspberry vinaigrette dressing
- 6 cups torn spinach leaves or romaine lettuce

1. Toss strawberries with apples, onions, cilantro and dressing in large bowl. Let stand 15 minutes.
2. Add spinach just before serving; mix lightly.

Servings: 6

Cooking Times

Preparation Time: 15 minutes
Cooking Time: 30 minutes
Total Time: 45 minutes

Strawberry Pretzel Salad

Pretzel Base

2 cups crushed pretzels
3/4 cup melted butter
3 tablespoons sugar

1. Preheat oven to 400 degrees F.
2. For the crust, mix the pretzels, butter, and 3 tablespoons of sugar. Press this mixture into a 9 by 13-inch pan and bake for 7 minutes. Set aside and allow to cool.

Gelatin Salad

3/4 cup sugar
1 8-ounce package cream cheese
1 8-ounce container frozen whipped topping
2 3-ounce packages strawberry gelatin
2 cups boiling water
2 10-ounce packages frozen strawberries
1 8-ounce can crushed pineapple
Whipped topping or whipped cream, to garnish

1. In a mixing bowl, beat together the cream cheese and 3/4 cup of sugar. Fold in the whipped topping, and spread over the cooled crust. Refrigerate until well chilled.
2. In a small bowl, dissolve the gelatin in the boiling water, and allow to cool slightly. Add the strawberries and pineapple, and pour over the cream cheese mixture. Refrigerate until serving time.
3. To serve, cut into slices and serve with a dollop of whipped topping.

Servings: 8

Cooking Times
Preparation Time: 30 minutes
Cooking Time: 10 minutes
Inactive Time: 2 minutes

Warm Spinach and McIntosh Apple Salad with Bacon

    4 thick bacon slices
    1 small red onion, sliced
    2 tablespoons cider vinegar
    2 teaspoons Dijon mustard
    1 teaspoon sugar
    Salt and pepper
    1 10-ounce bag fresh spinach rinsed and patted dry and torn into bite-size pieces
    1 McIntosh apple, cored and sliced thinly

1. In a skillet set over moderate heat cook the bacon until it is crisp.
2. Transfer the bacon to a plate lined with paper towel and let it drain.
3. Pour off all but 2 tablespoons fat from the skillet.
4. Add the onion to the skillet and cook it, stirring occasionally, for 3 minutes, or until it is wilted.
5. Add the vinegar, mustard, sugar and salt and pepper, to taste and bring the mixture to a boil, stirring.
6. In a serving bowl combine the spinach and apple.
7. Add the hot dressing and toss to combine and serve.

Servings: 6

Cooking Times
Preparation Time: 10 minutes
Total Time: 10 minutes

WILD BLUEBERRY VINAIGRETTE

1 cup fresh blueberries
¼ cup cider vinegar
¼ cup honey, or more to taste
2 tablespoons shallot, chopped
2 teaspoons Dijon mustard
½ teaspoon kosher salt
¼ teaspoon freshly ground pepper
1 cup canola oil

1. In a blender, combine blueberries, cider vinegar, honey, shallot, mustard, salt and pepper; blend until smooth. With blender running, gradually add oil in a slow, steady stream until emulsified.

2. Taste vinaigrette on a piece of salad green and adjust seasoning, if needed; may need additional honey depending on the ripeness or sweetness of the wild blueberries. Cover and refrigerate until serving.

Servings: 16
Yield: 2 cups

Yogurt Ranch Dressing

2 cups plain yogurt
1/4 to 1/2 cup really good mayonnaise
1/2 teaspoon EACH: garlic powder, onion powder, celery leaves, & salt
1/4 teaspoon EACH: pepper, paprika, & dill weed
1 teaspoon dry parsley, OR 2 tablespoons fresh chopped parsley

1. In a medium sized bowl, combine all of the ingredients. Mix it all very well, and allow it to marinate for several hours or overnight. If desired, add a dash of cayenne pepper.

2. Serve as a dip or dressing for salads.

Servings: 32
Yield: 2 1/4 cups

Cooking Times
Preparation Time: 10 minutes
Total Time: 10 minutes

Crossing the Three T's of Cooking

Salads & Dressings

Soups & Stews

There's nothing like homemade chicken noodle soup which is a lot easier to make than one might think. I make it the same way each time and freeze it to have on hand. If you don't have chicken on the bone then use frozen chicken breasts and grill them up with seasoning first and then make the soup. Soup made this way ends up with some great grilled flavor. An old standby is the six hour stew that you don't lift the lid while it is in the oven. Recently, my sister and family were in from out of state and I varied the recipe by adding tomato juice (they couldn't have seeds from tomatoes) and added some wine to enhance the base. Needless to say, we were licking the bowls. The mushroom soup is a favorite especially when made with portabella mushrooms.

Cream of Mushroom Soup

Beef Barley Soup with Red Wine and Roasted Garlic

1 medium red bell pepper seeded and chopped
1 medium onion chopped
10 cloves garlic, roasted and chopped
1 28-ounce can tomatoes stewed
1 tablespoon thyme chopped
1 tablespoon Worcestershire sauce
1 tablespoon horseradish
1/2 teaspoon black pepper
2 tablespoons olive oil
1 pound beef
2 medium carrots grated
1/2 cup red wine
6 cups beef stock
1/2 cup barley
1/2 cup basil, chopped
1/2 teaspoon sea salt

1. In a large soup pot, heat the oil. Add the beef, carrots, red pepper and onions, sauté for 4 minutes or until beef is browned.

2. Add the roasted garlic and wine; sauté until the liquid has evaporated, 2 to 3 minutes.

3. Add the tomatoes and their juice, stock, barley, basil, thyme, Worcestershire sauce, horseradish, salt and black pepper.

4. Bring to a boil; reduce heat and simmer another 10 to 12 minutes or until the barley is tender. Serve immediately.

Servings: 6

Cooking Times
Preparation Time: 20 minutes

Tips:
Seal garlic in aluminum foil to roast at 350° for 20 minutes. When they're done the skins will come off easily.

Cheddar Cheese Corn Chowder

2 potatoes peeled and cut into 1/2-inch cubes
1/2 cup carrots peeled and diced
1/2 cup celery chopped
1/2 cup onion chopped
1 teaspoon salt
1/4 teaspoon pepper
1/4 cup butter
2 tablespoons flour
4 cups milk
1 11-ounce can cream style corn
1 cup cheddar cheese grated

1. Place potatoes, carrots, celery, onion, salt and pepper in a pan.
2. Cover with water to cook. Cook for 15 minutes.
3. Add milk and cream style corn. Bring back to a boil.
4. Melt butter and add flour to make a paste.
5. Add to potato mixture to thicken the soup.
6. Add grated cheddar cheese. Bring back to boil.
7. Ladle into bowls and serve.

Servings: 4

Cooking Times
Preparation Time: 15 minutes
Cooking Time: 20 minutes
Total Time: 35 minutes

CHERRY CHILI

2 pounds ground beef chuck	1 1/3 cups chopped onion
1/2 cup chopped green bell pepper	1/3 cup chopped celery
2 cloves fresh garlic, minced	1 1/2 cups water
1 16-ounce can diced tomatoes	1 tablespoon tomato paste
1 15-ounce can tomato sauce	1 cup dried cherries
3 tablespoons chopped green chilies	2 tablespoons sugar
3 tablespoons chili powder	1/2 teaspoon pepper
1 teaspoon instant beef bouillon granules	1/2 teaspoon ground cumin
1 teaspoon bottled hot pepper sauce	1 bay leaf
1 15-ounce can kidney beans	1/3 cup beer

1. In a 4 to 5-quart Dutch oven or kettle, brown meat with onion, green pepper, celery, and garlic.

2. Add undrained tomatoes, tomato sauce, water, and tomato paste.

3. Stir in chili peppers, cherries, chili powder, sugar, bouillon, bottled hot-pepper sauce, pepper, cumin and bay leaf.

4. Add kidney beans.

5. Simmer uncovered, for 60 minutes, stirring often.

Servings: 10
Yield: 4 quarts

Cooking Times
Preparation Time: 15 minutes
Cooking Time: 1 hour
Total Time: 1 hour and 15 minutes

Corn Chowder with Sweet Potatoes and Ham

2 cups frozen or fresh corn

3 tablespoons unsalted butter

1/2 cup diced firm, baked smoked ham

2 1/2 cups finely chopped yellow onion

2 red bell peppers, seeded and diced

3 1/2 cups chicken broth

1 large sweet potato, about 1 pound. peeled and cut into 1/2-inch cubes

1 teaspoon salt, plus more, to taste

2/3 cup heavy cream

1/2 teaspoon hot-pepper sauce

1. In a soup pot over medium heat, melt the butter. Add the ham and cook, stirring once or twice, until lightly browned, about 10 minutes. Using a slotted spoon, transfer to a bowl.

2. Add the onion and bell peppers to the pot, cover and cook, stirring once or twice until tender, about 10 minutes.

3. Add the broth, sweet potato and the 1 teaspoon salt. Reduce the heat to low, partially cover and simmer for 10 minutes. Stir in the ham and corn kernels. Cover and cook until the potato is just tender, about 10 minutes.

4. Stir in the cream and hot-pepper sauce. Cook just until heated through, 3 to 4 minutes. Taste and adjust the seasonings. Serve hot.

Servings: 8

Cooking Times
Preparation Time: 15 minutes
Cooking Time: 30 minutes
Total Time: 45 minutes

CREAM OF BROCCOLI SOUP

1 pound fresh broccoli florets (or thawed frozen)
1/2 cup water
5 tablespoons butter, divided
1/2 medium onion, chopped
3 medium stalks celery chopped
4 tablespoons flour
2 14-ounce cans chicken broth
1/4 pound mushrooms, chopped
3 cups light cream
1 teaspoon salt
1/4 teaspoon white pepper
1 cup chopped ham
Grated cheddar cheese
1/4 teaspoon tarragon leaves, crushed

Servings: 12

Cooking Times
Preparation Time: 20 minutes
Cooking Time: 20 minutes
Total Time: 40 minutes

Continued on next page

Cream of Broccoli Soup

1. Cut broccoli into 1/2 inch slices, paring main stems and removing leaves.
2. In medium saucepan, combine broccoli pieces and water; steam, covered until tender, about 15 minutes.
3. Set pan aside; do not drain.
4. In large soup pot, melt four tablespoons of butter, add onion and celery; cook stirring frequently until soft, about six minutes.
5. Add flour and stir until thoroughly mixed; cook, stirring constantly until mixture is simmering and slightly thickened.
6. Add prepared broccoli and cooking water. Bring to a boil and simmer five minutes, stirring occasionally.
7. Melt remaining tablespoon of butter in small skillet.
8. Add chopped mushrooms and cook over high heat until moisture disappears.
9. Add to the soup pot with light cream, salt, white pepper and tarragon.
10. Heat slowly until hot, but do not boil. Stir in ham and serve a sprinkling of grated cheese on top.

CREAM OF MUSHROOM SOUP

4 tablespoons butter
1 onion finely chopped
1/2 pound mushrooms sliced
1/4 teaspoon basil, chopped
5 tablespoons flour
5 cups hot chicken stock
1/4 cup hot light cream
Juice of half a lemon
Dash paprika
Pinch celery seed
Pepper

1. Heat butter in saucepan. When hot, add onion, cover and cook 4 minutes over medium heat.

2. Add mushrooms, spices and lemon juice; mix well. Cover and cook 4 minutes over medium heat.

3. Mix in flour and cook 1 minute uncovered over low heat.

4. Pour in chicken stock and season, bring to boil. Cook soup uncovered, 12 minutes over medium heat.

5. Add cream. Puree soup in food processor, if desired.

6. Sprinkle with paprika and serve with croutons.

Servings: 4

Cream of Potato Soup

6 potatoes peeled and cut into 1/2-inch cubes
1 cup onion peeled and chopped
1 cup celery chopped
4 1/2 tablespoons butter
1 1/2 teaspoons salt
3 cups milk
3 cups water

1. Cover potatoes with water and bring to boil.

2. Add salt.

3. Sauté celery and onions in 1 1/2 tablespoons of butter, add to potatoes.

4. Melt 3 tablespoons of butter in sauté pan and add flour, paprika. It will look like a paste.

5. Add milk to potatoes and season to taste.

6. Add paste to hot potato mix and simmer for 10 minutes.

Servings: 6
Yield: 9 cups

Cooking Times
Preparation Time: 15 minutes
Cooking Time: 25 minutes
Total Time: 40 minutes

Tips:
I like to add chicken bouillon to potato mixture.
Use a wire whisk when adding paste to hot potato mixture.

CREAMY SQUASH SOUP

2 pounds butternut squash, halved, peeled, seeded, and cut into 1-inch pieces
1 1/2 cups diced onion
2 carrots, peeled and diced
3 13 3/4-ounce cans chicken broth
1/2 teaspoon salt
2 tablespoons butter
1/2 cup light cream or heavy cream
Sour cream, for garnish

1. In a medium saucepan, combine squash, onion, carrots, broth and salt. Simmer, uncovered, until squash is very tender, about 40 minutes.

2. Puree soup in a blender or food processor with the butter. Whisk cream into soup.

3. Serve in wide, shallow bowls with a dollop of sour cream, if desired.

Servings: 4

Cooking Times
Preparation Time: 15 minutes
Cooking Time: 40 minutes
Total Time: 55 minutes

Fantastic Black Bean Chili

1 tablespoon vegetable oil
1 onion diced
2 cloves fresh garlic, minced
1 pound ground turkey
3 15-ounce black beans, undrained
1 14-ounce crushed tomatoes
1 1/2 tablespoons chili powder
1 tablespoon dried oregano
1 tablespoon dried basil
1 tablespoon red wine vinegar

1. Heat the oil in a large heavy pan over medium heat.
2. Cook onion and garlic until onions are translucent.
3. Add turkey and cook, stirring until meat is brown.
4. Stir in beans, tomatoes, spices, and vinegar.
5. Reduce heat to low, cover and simmer 60 minutes or more.

Servings: 6

Cooking Times
Preparation Time: 20 minutes
Cooking Time: 1 hour and 15 minutes
Total Time: 1 hour and 35 minutes

FRENCH ONION SOUP

9 onions sliced
1 stick butter
1/2 teaspoon sugar
1/2 teaspoon salt
1 tablespoon flour
11 beef bouillon cubes
8 cups water
1/4 teaspoon Worcestershire sauce
1/4 teaspoon oregano
1/4 teaspoon pepper
1/4 teaspoon parsley flakes
Parmesan cheese
1 slice Swiss cheese
1/2 box croutons
1/4 teaspoon garlic powder

1. Simmer onions in 1 stick of butter until tender.

2. Add next 10 ingredients, mix well. Simmer 30 minutes.

3. Sprinkle parmesan cheese in and add croutons, top with Swiss cheese and sprinkle again with cheese.

4. Broil until brown and bubbly.

Servings: 6

Cooking Times

Preparation Time: 10 minutes
Cooking Time: 30 minutes
Total Time: 40 minutes

GAZPACHO

4 large tomatoes peeled and coarsely chopped
1 small cucumber, chopped
1 medium green pepper chopped
1 clove garlic clove, minced
3 cups tomato juice
1/4 cup wine vinegar
1 1/2 teaspoons instant chicken bouillon granules
1/2 teaspoon pepper
Few dashes bottled hot pepper sauce

1. In a large mixing bowl combine tomatoes, cucumber, green pepper, onion, and garlic.
2. Stir in tomato juice, wine vinegar, bouillon granules, pepper, and hot pepper sauce.
3. Cover and chill several hours.

Servings: 10

Cooking Times
Preparation Time: 15 minutes
Inactive Time: 2 hours
Total Time: 2 hours and 15 minutes

Mom's Chicken Noodle Soup

    3 chicken breasts
    6 carrots peeled and thinly sliced
    4 stalks celery cut into 1/4-inch cubes
    4 teaspoons chicken bouillon granules
    1 package noodles

1. Pan grill the chicken breasts with seasonings of choice (salt & pepper or chicken rub seasoning).

2. Cut up in chunks and set aside.

3. Boil cut up carrots and celery with chicken bouillon granules in 2 quarts of water.

4. When still a little bit crunchy, add the cut up chicken and noodles.

5. Bring to a boil.

6. Taste to see if additional seasoning needed. You also may add more water depending on the consistency that you like the soup.

7. Simmer until noodles are tender.

Servings: 10

Cooking Times
Preparation Time: 15 minutes
Cooking Time: 30 minutes
Total Time: 45 minutes

OVEN STEW POT

1 14-ounce can chopped tomato undrained
4 carrots
1/2 cup Tapioca; quick-cooking
2 teaspoons salt
Pepper to taste
1 onion chopped
3 potatoes, peeled and cubed
2 1/2 pound beef chuck roast cut up
1can green beans with water
3 stalks celery cut into 1/4-inch cubes

1. Mix all ingredients together, place in oven proof Dutch oven pan with lid.
2. Put in 250° oven for 6 hours.
3. Do not peek during slow cooking process.
4. Serve warm.

Oven Temperature: 250°F

Servings: 6

Cooking Times
Preparation Time: 20 minutes
Cooking Time: 6 hours
Total Time: 6 hours and 20 minutes

Tips:
Use tomato juice and tomato soup if you prefer no seeds in the sauce.

PUMPKIN AND BEAN SOUP

   1 15-ounce can pumpkin
   1 15-ounce can white kidney beans
   1 15-ounce can unsweetened coconut milk
   1 15-ounce can vegetable broth
   Salt and pepper, to taste
   1 teaspoon dried sage
   Fresh lime slices

1. Mix pumpkin, beans, milk, broth, salt, pepper, and sage. Heat thoroughly.

2. Serve warm with lime slices.

Servings: 4
Yield: 58 ounces

Stuffed Bell Pepper Soup

2 tablespoons olive oil
1 tablespoon minced garlic
2 cups chopped onion
3 large green bell peppers, chopped
2 14-ounce cans sliced stewed tomatoes
1 pound ground beef
1 8-ounce can tomato paste

2 cups cooked brown rice
1/2 teaspoon Cajun spice
1 teaspoon basil
1 tablespoon parsley flakes
1/4 cup soy sauce
1/4 cup red wine

1. Brown hamburger in pan. Season the hamburger with the minced garlic.
2. Drain it, set aside.
3. Add the olive oil to the pan and chopped bell peppers.
4. Cook the peppers until they start to wilt.
5. Add the hamburger back to the pan with the peppers.
6. Add the tomato paste, 1 can water and the 2 cans of tomatoes.
7. After the tomato paste is dissolved, add the Cajun spice, basil, parsley, soy sauce and red wine.
8. When it starts to boil, add 2 cups brown 10 minute rice or already cooked rice.
9. Let it cook for 10 minutes.

Servings: 6

Cooking Times
Preparation Time: 10 minutes
Cooking Time: 10 minutes
Total Time: 20 minutes

TACO SOUP

1 32-ounce jar northern beans
1 11-ounce can diced tomatoes
2 cans drained corn
1 package Taco seasoning mix

1. Mix all ingredients and cook until done.

Servings: 6
Yield: 3 quarts

Cooking Times
Preparation Time: 10 minutes
Cooking Time: 45 minutes
Total Time: 55 minutes

Tips:
Add water if you like the soup thinner.
Serve the soup with tortilla strips and sour cream.

White Chicken Chili

1 11-ounce can chicken breast
1 32-ounce jar of great northern white beans
1/2 15-ounce jar of salsa
2 11-ounce cans chicken broth
1 tablespoon cumin
2 cups Colby cheese
2 cups crushed tortilla chips

1. Place chicken, beans, salsa, chicken broth, cumin, and cheese in large pot.
2. Heat on medium until cheese is melted.
3. Add crushed corn chips as topping.

Servings: 8
Yield: 76 ounces

Crossing the Three T's of Cooking

Soups & Stews

Vegetables

My family's favorite vegetable is probably corn, but they do enjoy some of the other vegetable dishes I have included because there may be a sauce or a little twist on an old favorite. One in particular is the grilled vegetables with the basil sauce which was served for a Sunday afternoon cookout. I went overboard on the grilled vegetables and had so many leftover that my husband and I made a grilled vegetable pizza with a creamy Alfredo sauce the next night. Yum Yum! The Au Gratin potatoes are great baked up in an oblong baking dish or scooped into little ramekins for individual portions. The Brandied Mushrooms are an excellent addition to any meat either out of the oven or off the grill. My brother used to love my Escalloped Corn and asked that I bring it to all the family gatherings. Try the little Potato and Onion pockets; they'll remind you of your camping experiences. I grew up eating fried green tomatoes. They tasted so good but most of the times were a little greasy and soggy. This baked recipe makes them crispy so that you can pick them up and eat them with your hands. Serve with mayonnaise mixed with pickle relish and a little horseradish. The Winter Vegetable Medley is a wonderful blend of vegetables and is dressed out for the holidays. The last time I served this, my grandson's friend stopped by for a bite to eat. He couldn't get enough of our food but wanted to especially know how these vegetables were made. Turns out, he loved to cook and appreciated tasty food.

Grilled Vegetables

AU GRATIN POTATOES

    6 cups potatoes diced
    1/2 cup butter (no substitutes)
    1/4 cup flour
    2 cups milk
    1/2 teaspoon salt
    1/4 teaspoon pepper
    1 teaspoon paprika
    1 teaspoon chicken bouillon granules
    6 ounces block processed cheese cubed

1. Prepare potatoes.

2. Melt butter in large sauce pan.

3. Add flour and blend.

4. Gradually add milk and cook until thick.

5. Add remaining ingredients and stir until cheese melts and sauce is smooth.

6. Stir in potatoes and pour into casserole dish.

7. Bake uncovered at 350° for 25-30 minutes until top is browned.

8. May top with soft bread crumbs.

Oven Temperature: 350°F

Servings: 6

Cooking Times
Preparation Time: 45 minutes
Cooking Time: 30 minutes
Total Time: 1 hour and 15 minutes

BRANDIED MUSHROOMS

3 pounds fresh mushrooms, sliced lengthwise
8 tablespoons butter
Seasoning salt
1/4 cup Worcestershire sauce
1/2 cup brandy

1. In a large skillet, sauté the sliced mushrooms in the butter until brown. Sprinkle liberally with seasoning salt.

2. Add Worcestershire sauce and simmer until almost all sauce is absorbed by the mushrooms.

3. Add the brandy and continue to simmer until mushrooms are tender.

4. Serve with steak or roast beef.

Servings: 4

Cooking Times
Preparation Time: 10 minutes
Cooking Time: 20 minutes

BROCCOLI CASSEROLE

2 10-ounce frozen packages chopped broccoli, cooked and drained
1 cup mayonnaise
1 cup grated cheddar cheese
1 10 3/4-ounce can condensed cream of mushroom soup
2 eggs, lightly beaten
2 cups crushed crackers
2 tablespoons butter, melted

1. Preheat oven to 350°. Spray a 13 x 9 inch baking dish with cooking spray.

2. In a large mixing bowl, combine broccoli, mayonnaise, cheese, soup and eggs. Mix well with a metal spoon.

3. Place mixture in the prepared baking dish. Top with crushed crackers and pour the melted butter evenly over the crackers.

4. Bake for 35 minutes or until set and browned.

Oven Temperature: 350°F

Servings: 8

Cooking Times
Preparation Time: 10 minutes
Cooking Time: 35 minutes
Total Time: 45 minutes

Easy Spinach Quiche

1 unbaked 10-inch pie crust
1/2 cup grated cheddar or Gruyere cheese
4 eggs, beaten
1 cup reduced fat milk
1 13.5-ounce can spinach, well drained
1/4 cup bacon bits
1 roma tomato, thinly sliced

1. Preheat oven to 425°F.
2. Prepare crust according to package directions.
3. Sprinkle cheese on pie crust.
4. Mix eggs, milk, spinach, and bacon bits; pour mixture evenly over cheese.
5. Top with slices of tomato.
6. Bake 15 minutes; reduce heat to 350 degrees F and bake an additional 20 to 25 minutes until set, or a toothpick inserted in center comes out clean.
7. Remove from oven and let stand 10 minutes.
8. Cut into slices and serve warm.

Oven Temperature: 425°F

Servings: 4

ESCALLOPED CORN

2 cups frozen corn, thawed and drained
1 cup cracker crumbs
1/4 cup chopped onions
1/2 cup chopped celery
2/3 cup grated cheddar cheese
1 teaspoon salt
2 beaten eggs
1 1/2 cups milk
2 tablespoons melted butter

1. Crumb crackers.
2. Chop celery, onion.
3. Grate cheese.
4. Beat eggs and mix with milk and melted butter.
5. Mix all ingredients together and place in buttered dish.
6. Bake 1 hour at 350° or until a knife inserted in the center comes out clean.

Oven Temperature: 350°F

Servings: 10

Cooking Times
Preparation Time: 20 minutes
Cooking Time: 1 hour
Total Time: 1 hour and 20 minutes

Giant Potato Pancakes

2 eggs
4 medium potatoes peeled and grated
1 medium onion chopped
1 teaspoon salt
1/8 teaspoon pepper
1/4 teaspoon nutmeg
3 tablespoons flour

1. Beat eggs slightly in large bowl.
2. Peel and grate potatoes into bowl with eggs. Stir occasionally while grating to coat potatoes with eggs to prevent darkening. Grate onion into bowl with potato mixture, then stir in salt, pepper, nutmeg and enough flour to make batter hold together.
3. Heat 2 tablespoons oil in shallow 10-inch skillet until almost sizzling. Pour in half the batter, about 2 cups and spread quickly to the sides of the pan. Cook over medium heat until well-browned on the underside.
4. Lift carefully with spatula to check brownness. Slide pancake onto a plate, cover with another plate and flip over so the cooked side is uppermost. Slide back into pan and brown the other side. Turn onto plate. Cool the pancake. Cut pancakes into wedges and serve with applesauce.

Servings: 4

Cooking Times
Preparation Time: 15 minutes

Tips:

Use this batter to make smaller pancakes which will cook faster. Just drop the batter by large spoonfuls into hot oil and brown well on each side.

Serve the pancakes with butter, sour cream, and applesauce.

GRILLED POTATO AND ONION PACKAGES

2/3 cup olive oil
1 tablespoon Dijon mustard
2 tablespoons chopped fresh thyme or 1 tablespoon dried
1 teaspoon salt
1 teaspoon ground black pepper
2 pounds white-skinned potatoes (about 4 large), peeled, sliced 1/4 inch thick
2 large red onions, halved, sliced 1/2 inch thick
Nonstick vegetable oil spray
Fresh thyme sprigs (optional)

Servings: 6

Cooking Times
Preparation Time: 15 minutes
Cooking Time: 8 minutes
Total Time: 23 minutes

Tips:

Turn foil pockets over during grilling.

Continued on next page

Grilled Potato and Onion Packages

1. Combine oil, mustard, thyme, salt and pepper in large bowl. Whisk to blend well. (Can be prepared 6 hours ahead. Cover and let stand at room temperature.)

2. Prepare the grill (medium-high heat). Add potatoes and onions to mustard oil. Toss to coat.

3. Set six 18 x 9-inch sheets of heavy-duty aluminum foil on work surface. Spray foil with nonstick vegetable oil spray.

4. Divide vegetables among foil sheets, placing in center of left half of each. Sprinkle with salt and pepper.

5. Fold right half of foil over vegetables. Fold edges of packages together to seal tightly.

6. Place packages on grill. Grill until potatoes are tender and golden brown, turning occasionally, about 25 minutes.

7. Remove packages from grill. Slit top of foil and fold back.

8. Garnish potatoes with thyme sprigs, if desired.

GRILLED RAINBOW PEPPERS

3 bell peppers (1 each of red, green, yellow. Small ones are very nice)
Vegetable cooking spray
3 tablespoons olive oil
2 tablespoons balsamic vinegar
1 tablespoon brown sugar
1/2 cup goat cheese
Fresh basil
Salt and pepper to taste

1. Quarter bell peppers and lightly coat with vegetable spray.

2. Grill peppers, covered with grill lid for 5 minutes on each side or until tender.

3. Arrange, cut sides up on a serving platter.

4. Whisk together olive oil, balsamic vinegar and brown sugar. Drizzle over peppers.

5. Sprinkle with crumbled goat cheese, basil, and salt and pepper.

Servings: 4

Cooking Times
Preparation Time: 10 minutes
Cooking Time: 10 minutes
Total Time: 20 minutes

GRILLED VEGETABLES

3 yellow squash (about 1 pound total), sliced lengthwise into 1/2-inch-thick rectangles
3 zucchini (about 12 ounces total), sliced lengthwise into 1/2-inch-thick rectangles
3 Japanese eggplant (12 ounces total), sliced lengthwise into 1/2-inch-thick rectangles
12 mushrooms
1 bunch (1-pound) asparagus, trimmed
12 green onions, roots cut off
1/4 cup plus 2 tablespoons olive oil
Salt and freshly ground black pepper
3 tablespoons balsamic vinegar
2 garlic cloves, minced
1 teaspoon chopped fresh Italian parsley leaves
1 teaspoon chopped fresh basil leaves
1/2 teaspoon finely chopped fresh rosemary leaves

Servings: 6

Cooking Times
Preparation Time: 15 minutes
Cooking Time: 25 minutes

Continued on next page

GRILLED VEGETABLES

1. Place a grill pan over medium-high heat or prepare the barbecue (medium-high heat). Brush the vegetables with 1/4 cup of the oil to coat lightly.

2. Grill the vegetables until tender and lightly charred all over, about 8 to 10 minutes for the bell peppers; 7 minutes for the yellow squash, zucchini, eggplant, and mushrooms; 4 minutes for the asparagus and green onions.

3. Sprinkle the vegetables with salt and pepper. Arrange the vegetables on a platter.

4. Meanwhile, whisk the remaining 2 tablespoons of oil, balsamic vinegar, garlic, parsley, basil, and rosemary in a small bowl to blend. Add salt and pepper to taste. Drizzle the herb mixture over the vegetables.

5. Serve the vegetables, warm or at room temperature.

Hash Brown Casserole

2 pounds frozen hash browns
1 10 ¾ ounce can cream of mushroom soup
2 cups grated cheddar cheese
1 pint sour cream
1/2 cup chopped onion
1 teaspoon salt
Pepper to taste
1/2 cup butter (optional)

1. Mix all ingredients and place in a 9 x 13 pan and bake at 350° for 45 minutes.

Oven Temperature: 350°F

Servings: 10

Cooking Times
Preparation Time: 10 minutes
Cooking Time: 45 minutes
Total Time: 55 minutes

Homemade Cripsy Seasoned French Fries

2 1/2 pounds russet potatoes, peeled
1 cup all-purpose flour
1 teaspoon garlic salt
1 teaspoon onion salt
1 teaspoon salt
1 teaspoon paprika
1/2 cup water, or as needed
1 cup vegetable oil for frying

1. Slice potatoes into French fries, and place into cold water so they won't turn brown while you prepare the oil.

2. Heat oil in a large skillet over medium-high heat. While the oil is heating, sift the flour, garlic salt, onion salt, (regular) salt, and paprika into a large bowl. Gradually stir in enough water so that the mixture can be drizzled from a spoon.

3. Dip potato slices into the batter one at a time, and place in the hot oil so they are not touching at first. The fries must be placed into the skillet one at a time, or they will clump together. Fry until golden brown and crispy.

4. Remove and drain on paper towels.

Servings: 8

Cooking Times
Preparation Time: 15 minutes
Cooking Time: 10 minutes

Mashed Potatoes with Ranch Dressing

Dressing

1/2 cup buttermilk
1/2 cup mayonnaise
3 tablespoons chives, snipped or onion, minced
3 tablespoons parsley
1/2 teaspoon garlic salt
1/2 teaspoon onion powder
1/4 teaspoon black pepper

1. Make dressing by mixing all ingredients, refrigerate.

Potatoes

5 to 6 pounds russet potatoes
1 tablespoon kosher salt
3/4 cup whipping cream
1/2 cup whole milk
1/4 cup butter

1. Cook potatoes for about 20 minutes. Drain. Let stand 20 minutes.

2. Combine cream, milk, butter; fold half of mixture into potatoes. Repeat with rest of cream.

3. Fold 3/4 ranch dressing into potatoes. Check consistency. Fold remaining dressing in.

4. You may keep potatoes warm at 350° oven for 30 minutes.

Servings: 6

Cooking Times
Preparation Time: 15 minutes
Cooking Time: 20 minutes
Inactive Time: 20 minutes
Total Time: 55 minutes

Oven Baked Sweet Potato Fries

1/2 teaspoon ground cumin
1/2 teaspoon salt
1/4 teaspoon ground red pepper
1 tablespoon vegetable oil
2 large sweet potatoes, peeled and sliced in wedges

Prepare the sweet potatoes:

1. In a small bowl, combine cumin, salt and pepper. Set aside.
2. Preheat oven to 400°.
3. Peel potatoes, cut each in half lengthwise, and cut each half in 6 wedges.
4. In a large bowl, combine the cut potatoes, oil, and spicy mixture.
5. Toss until potatoes are evenly coated.

Bake the fries:

1. On a baking sheet, arrange potatoes in a single layer and place on middle shelf of the oven.
2. Bake until edges are crisp and potatoes are cooked through, about 30 minutes.
3. Serve immediately.

Oven Temperature: 400°F

Servings: 4

Cooking Times
Preparation Time: 10 minutes
Inactive Time: 30 minutes
Total Time: 40 minutes

OVEN FRIED GREEN TOMATOES

4 to 6 green tomatoes cut in 1/4-inch thick slices
2 eggs, beaten
2/3 cup evaporated milk
1/3 cup water
Salt and pepper
1 1/2 cups all-purpose flour

1. Sprinkle tomato slices with salt and pepper on both sides. In a shallow bowl mix beaten eggs, milk, and water. Put the all-purpose flour in a shallow bowl. Dip each slice into egg mixture, then into flour. Dip each slice into egg and then into the flour again. Arrange tomatoes in large, shallow, greased baking pans, or bake in one pan, in batches. Tomatoes should not touch.

2. Bake uncovered in 400° oven 20 minutes, turning halfway through.

3. For crunchier coating, dip slices the second time into egg mixture then into seasoned bread crumbs or corn flake crumbs, with a little Parmesan cheese, if desired.

Oven Temperature: 400°F

Servings: 4

Cooking Times
Preparation Time: 20 minutes
Cooking Time: 20 minutes

TOMATO PIE

1 9-inch frozen pie shell, thawed
3 large tomatoes, about 1 1/2 pounds, cut into 1/2-inch-thick slices
Kosher salt, for sprinkling
1/4 cup Dijon mustard
1 cup coarsely grated Gruyere
1 tablespoon finely chopped fresh parsley leaves
1 tablespoon chopped fresh thyme leaves
1 garlic clove, minced
2 tablespoons extra-virgin olive oil
Additional kosher salt and freshly ground black pepper

Oven Temperature: 400°F

Servings: 6

Cooking Times
Preparation Time: 45 minutes
Cooking Time: 1 hour

Tips:
Use crescent rolls for pie crust.

Continued on next page

Tomato Pie

1. Preheat the oven to 375 degrees F.

2. Line the shell with foil and fill with pie weights, dried beans, or rice. Bake in the lower third of the oven for 20 minutes. Carefully remove the weights and foil. Return to the oven and bake for 10 minutes more or until light golden. Cool in the pan on a wire rack.

3. Turn up the oven to 400 degrees F.

4. Sprinkle the tomatoes with salt and drain in a colander for 10 to 15 minutes. Spread the mustard over the bottom of the shell and sprinkle the cheese over it. Arrange the tomatoes over the cheese in 1 overlapping layer. Bake until the pastry is golden brown and the tomatoes are very soft, 35 to 40 minutes.

5. In a small bowl, stir together the parsley, thyme, garlic, olive oil, and salt and pepper to taste to blend. Sprinkle the pie with this mixture while hot and spread out gently with the back of a spoon. Serve the pie hot or at room temperature.

Winter Medley with Garlic Basil Sauce

Vegetable Medley

1 10-ounce package frozen broccoli spears
1 10-ounce package frozen Brussels sprouts
16 baby carrots
1 medium zucchini, sliced
1 20-ounce can pearl onions

1. Cook frozen vegetables in separate saucepans, using package directions. Drain.
2. Cook carrots and zucchini in water to cover in separate saucepans just until crisp tender. Drain.
3. Heat onions in saucepan.

Servings: 8

Cooking Times
Preparation Time: 5 minutes
Cooking Time: 10 minutes
Total Time: 15 minutes

Continued on next page

WINTER MEDLEY WITH GARLIC BASIL SAUCE

Garlic and Basil Sauce

1/2 cup olive oil
2 tablespoons lemon juice
2 teaspoons grated lemon rind
2 cloves garlic chopped
1/4 cup chopped parsley
1 teaspoon dried basil leaves
1 teaspoon salt
1/2 teaspoon pepper

1. Combine olive oil, lemon juice, lemon rind, garlic, parsley, basil, salt and pepper in small covered container, shake to mix well.
2. Arrange vegetables on serving plate. Pour Garlic and Basil Sauce over warm vegetables just before serving.

Yellow Squash Casserole

4 cups sliced yellow squash
1/2 cup chopped onion
35 buttery round crackers, crushed
1 cup shredded Cheddar cheese
Ground black pepper to taste

2 eggs, beaten
3/4 cup milk
1/4 cup butter, melted
1 teaspoon salt
2 tablespoons butter

1. Preheat oven to 400 degrees F.

2. Place squash and onion in a large skillet over medium heat. Pour in a small amount of water. Cover, and cook until squash is tender, about 5 minutes. Drain well, and place in a large bowl.

3. In a medium bowl, mix together cracker crumbs and cheese. Stir half of the cracker mixture into the cooked squash and onions. In a small bowl, mix together eggs and milk, then add to squash mixture.

4. Stir in 1/4 cup melted butter, and season with salt and pepper. Spread into a 9x13 inch baking dish. Sprinkle with remaining cracker mixture, and dot with 2 tablespoons butter.

5. Bake in preheated oven for 25 minutes, or until lightly browned.

Oven Temperature: 400°F

Servings: 10

Cooking Times
Preparation Time: 20 minutes
Cooking Time: 30 minutes
Total Time: 50 minutes

Zucchini Alfredo

- 5 large zucchini, unpeeled, and cut in 1/2 inch slices
- 1 teaspoon salt
- 2 to 3 cloves garlic, minced
- 2 tablespoons olive oil
- 1 8-ounce package cream cheese
- 3/4 cup half and half cream
- 1/2 cup grated parmesan cheese
- Coarsely ground black pepper
- Ground nutmeg

1. Cut zucchini in half crosswise. Cut lengthwise into 1/4 inch slices, and then lengthwise into long, thin strips about 1/4 inch wide (resembling strips of fettuccine). You should have about 8 cups. In a large colander toss the zucchini with the salt. Allow to drain for 1 hour. Rinse and drain; pat dry.

2. In a 12-inch skillet cook the zucchini and garlic in hot oil over medium high heat for 2 to 4 minutes or until crisp tender. Transfer mixture from skillet to a large bowl.

3. In the skillet heat the cream cheese. Stir in zucchini, heat through. Transfer to a serving dish. Sprinkle with pepper, nutmeg, and additional Parmesan cheese.

Servings: 8

Cooking Times
Preparation Time: 15 minutes
Cooking Time: 4 minutes
Inactive Time: 1 hour
Total Time: 1 hour and 19 minutes

Crossing the Three T's of Cooking

Index of Recipes

ABC PIE (APPLE, BLUEBERRY, AND CHERRY)	132
ABSOLUTELY WONDERFUL GREEK DRESSING	160
ACKNOWLEDGEMENTS	i
AMBROSIA SALAD	131
ANN'S RAISIN SQUARE	133
APPETIZERS & SNACKS	3
APPLE HARVEST CAKE	34
ASPARAGUS PESTO	4
AU GRATIN POTATOES	206
AWESOME CHEESECAKE	35
BAKED BEEF STROGANOFF	94
BAKED CHICKEN BREASTS SUPREME	144
BAKLAVA	54
BARBECUE RIBS IN SLOW COOKER	95
BEEF BARLEY SOUP WITH RED WINE AND ROASTED GARLIC	186
BETTY'S POLISH SAUSAGE AND SAUERKRAUT	96
BLACK BEAN SALAD	162
BLACK BEAN SALSA	5
BLENDER MAYONNAISE	163
BRAISED BEEF SHORT RIBS	97
BRANDIED MUSHROOMS	207
BREAD PUDDING WITH LEMON SAUCE	70
BREAD STICKS	16
BREADS	15
BRINE FOR SMOKED SALMON	88

BRINE FOR TURKEY	145
BROCCOLI CASSEROLE	208
BROWN SUGAR CHRISTMAS COOKIES	55
BUTTERNUT SQUASH WITH HERBED RICE	116
BUTTERSCOTCH BROWNIES	56
CAKES	33
CAPPUCCINO MOUSSE TRIFLE	71
CARAMEL CRUNCH	6
CARAMEL GLAZE FOR STICKY BUNS	36
CAROL'S PEANUT BUTTER CRISSCROSSES	57
CARROT CAKE DRIED FRUIT RING	37
CARROT SALAD	164
CEREAL COOKIES	58
CHEDDAR CHEESE CORN CHOWDER	187
CHEESE BALL	7
CHEESE STUFFED SHELLS	118
CHERRY CHILI	188
CHICKEN AND BISCUITS CASSEROLE	146
CHICKEN POT PIE	147
CHOCOLATE-PEANUT BUTTER PUDDING	72
CINNAMON ROLLS	17
CLASSIC MACARONI SALAD	119
COCONUT BUTTERBALLS	59
COD CAKES	89
COLESLAW DRESSING	165
COOKIES	53
COOL RISE HONEY LEMON WHOLE WHEAT BREADS	18
CORN CHOWDER WITH SWEET POTATOES AND	

Index of Recipes

HAM	189
CRAB MEAT SPREAD	8
CRANBERRY CHICKEN	148
CREAM OF BROCCOLI SOUP	190
CREAM OF MUSHROOM SOUP	192
CREAM OF POTATO SOUP	193
CREAMY SQUASH SOUP	194
CRISPY OATMEAL COOKIES	60
CRUNCHY CHRISTMAS RICE	120
CUP CAKES	38
DANISH RICE PUDDING	73
DEEP DISH APPLE PIE	134
DESSERTS	69
DILL PARMESAN POPOVERS	19
EASY OVERNIGHT CINNAMON ROLLS	20
EASY SPINACH QUICHE	209
EGG CASSEROLE	84
EGGS, CHEESE, LEGUMES	83
ENCHILADAS	99
ESCALLOPED CORN	210
ESTHER'S PERFECT APPLE PIE	135
FANTASTIC BLACK BEAN CHILI	195
FESTIVE ALMOND ICE CREAM BALLS	74
FETTUCCINE ALFREDO	121
FILET MIGNONS WITH MUSHROOM MADEIRA SAUCE	101
FISH & SHELLFISH	87
FISH CASSEROLE	90
FLUFFY FRUIT SALAD	166

FRENCH DRESSING	167
FRENCH ONION SOUP	196
FRESH BLUEBERRY PIE	136
FRESH BROCCOLI SALAD	168
FRESH PEACH PIE	137
FRESH RHUBARB PIE	138
FRESH STRAWBERRY PIE	139
FRUIT DIP	9
FRUITY HORSERADISH CREAM CHEESE	10
GAZPACHO	197
GERMAN CHOCOLATE CAKE WITH COCONUT-PECAN FROSTING	39
GIANT POTATO PANCAKES	211
GINGER CRINKLES	61
GLORIFIED RICE	75
GOLDEN GLAZED TURKEY WITH SAUSAGE AND MUSHROOM STUFFING AND PERFECT TURKEY GRAVY	149
GOLDFISH (SALMON) CAKES	91
GRANDMA CONLIN'S SLUMGULLION FRUIT SALAD	169
GRANDMA'S ROLLS	21
GRANOLA	122
GREEN PARTY RYE BITES	11
GRILLED POTATO AND ONION PACKAGES	212
GRILLED RAINBOW PEPPERS	214
GRILLED VEGETABLES	215
HASH BROWN CASSEROLE	217
HOMEMADE BUTTERMILK RANCH DRESSING	170
HOMEMADE CRISPY SEASONED FRENCH FRIES	218
HOT ARTICHOKE DIP	12

Index of Recipes

HOT CHICKEN SALAD	171
INTRODUCTION	1
LASAGNA, SHORT CUT STYLE	123
LIME GELATIN DESSERT	76
LIMONCELLO CHEESECAKE SQUARES	77
LOBSTER (IMITATION CRAB MEAT) MACARONI AND CHEESE	124
LUSCIOUS FOUR-LAYER PUMPKIN CAKE	41
MAPLE FROSTING	42
MARGIE'S SAUERKRAUT SALAD	172
MARY'S POTATO SALAD	173
MASHED POTATOES WITH RANCH DRESSING	219
MAYONNAISE CRUSTED CHICKEN	151
MEAT	93
MINI BLACK FOREST CAKES	43
MOLASSES COOKIES	62
MOM'S CHICKEN NOODLE SOUP	198
MORNING PECAN CASSEROLE	85
NEW YORK STYLE REUBEN SANDWICH	102
NO BAKE COOKIES	63
OATMEAL CAKE	44
OLD FASHIONED EGG BREAD	22
OLD FASHIONED MAC AND CHEESE	126
OLD FASHIONED STAINED GLASS CAKE	78
ORANGE CAULIFLOWER SALAD	174
ORIENTAL SALAD	175
OUT TO THE FARM FRIED STEAK WITH BISCUITS AND GRAVY	103
OVEN BAKED SWEET POTATO FRIES	220

OVEN FRIED GREEN TOMATOES	221
OVEN STEW POT	199
OVERNIGHT FRENCH TOAST	23
PASTA, RICE AND GRAINS	115
PATTY'S SOUR CREAM COOKIES	64
PEPPER STEAK	105
PERFECT CHOCOLATE CHIP COOKIES	65
PIES	131
PISTACHIO CAKE	45
PIZZA NIGHT PIZZA DOUGH	25
PORK WITH RED PLUM SAUCE	106
POULTRY	143
PUFFED OVEN PANCAKE WITH APPLE RAISIN SAUCE	26
PUMPKIN AND BEAN SOUP	200
PUMPKIN COOKIES	66
PUMPKIN PIE	140
PUMPKIN ROLL	46
RASPBERRY WALNUT TORTE	79
RESTAURANT QUALITY FRIED RICE	127
RESTAURANT QUALITY ORANGE CHICKEN	152
REUBEN CASSEROLE	107
RHUBARB COBBLER	80
RUM BALLS	67
RUSSIAN SALAD DRESSING	176
SALADS & DRESSINGS	159
SALISBURY STEAK WITH MASHED POTATOES	109
SALSA	13
SAUSAGE AND PECAN DRESSING CASSEROLE	154

Index of Recipes

SEVEN-LAYER SALAD	177
SLOPPY JOES	110
SMOKED TURKEY	155
SMOKY EGGPLANT DIP	14
SOUPS & STEWS	185
SPAGHETTI PIE	129
SPECIAL OCCASION GLAZED FRUIT	81
SPINACH AND STRAWBERRY SALAD	178
STACKED HAMBURGER CHILI RICE BOWLS	111
STRAWBERRY APPLE SALSA SALAD	179
STRAWBERRY PRETZEL SALAD	180
STRAWBERRY RHUBARB COFFEE CAKE	47
STUFFED BELL PEPPER SOUP	201
SUGAR COOKIE DOUGH	68
SWEET AND SOUR PORK	112
SWEET DOUGH FOR GERMAN APPLESAUCE CAKE	27
SWEET POTATO PIE	141
SWEET POTATO STUFFING WITH BACON AND THYME	156
SWISS CHEESE AND MUSHROOM QUICHE	86
TABLE OF CONTENTS	iii
TACO SOUP	202
TERRIFIC HAMBURGER BUNS	28
TEXAS SHEET CAKE WITH FUDGE FROSTING	49
TOMATO PIE	222
TURKEY APPLE SAUSAGE	157
VALENTINE CHERRY SCONES	29
VEGETABLES	205
WAKKY-KAKE	50

WARM SPINACH AND MCINTOSH APPLE SALAD WITH BACON	181
WHITE CHICKEN CHILI	203
WHOLE WHEAT HEARTINESS BREAD	30
WILD BLUEBERRY VINAIGRETTE	182
WINTER MEDLEY WITH GARLIC BASIL SAUCE	224
WONDROUS WAFFLES	31
YELLOW SQUASH CASSEROLE	226
YOGURT RANCH DRESSING	183
ZUCCHINI ALFREDO	227
ZUCCHINI BREAD	32
ZUCCHINI CAKE	51